DOCTORS DEVILS SAINTS AND SINNERS

JAMES BRIDIE

DOCTORS DEVILS SAINTS AND SINNERS

A Critical Study of the Major Plays of
JAMES BRIDIE

JOHN THOMAS LOW

THE RAMSAY HEAD PRESS EDINBURGH

First published in 1980 by
The Ramsay Head Press
36 North Castle Street
Edinburgh EH2 3BN
ISBN 0 902859 59 5

Printed in Great Britain by
Macdonald Printers (Edinburgh) Limited
Loanhead.

The publisher acknowledges the
financial assistance of the
Scottish Arts Council in the
publication of this volume.

Contents

THE MAIN PART of this work consists of a study of nine of Bridie's major plays designed to demonstrate his qualities and skill as a dramatist and the characteristics that mark him as a Scottish writer. These nine plays are not arranged chronologically but in groups according to subject matter or common characteristics. The first chapter deals with three of Bridie's doctor plays—*The Anatomist, A Sleeping Clergyman,* and *Dr. Angelus,* placed together not only because they are studies of medical life, but also because in their varying ways they reflect an idealist quality, that search for a medical Holy Grail. The second chapter groups together two biblical plays *Tobias and the Angel* and *Susannah and the Elders* which are linked by their common origin—the Apocrypha, and by a characteristic combination of the devotional and the human. In the third chapter there are studies of two of Bridie's portrait dramas—*Mr. Bolfry* and *Mr. Gillie,* contrasting pieces that illustrate Bridie's interest in professional people. The two late experimental plays *Daphne Laureola* and *The Baikie Charivari* are brought together in the fourth chapter: there is a contrast here in subject matter but a similarity in method. Bridie in these works is developing his dramatic use of symbolism, myth and legend.

In the second part of the work an attempt is made to estimate Bridie's skill as a dramatist, as a craftsman in language, and as a Scottish writer. In Chapter Five his structural methods and dramatic devices are examined; in Chapter Six his versatility in handling language is illustrated; and in the final chapter an attempt is made to indicate some of the qualities that give him a place in the history of Scottish literature and in European drama of the twentieth century.

Of the works consulted I have found three particularly valuable. Helen L. Luyben's study *James Bridie: Clown and Philosopher* is full of shrewd judgments and illuminating commentary. Ursula Gerber's published thesis (in German) *James Bridies Dramen* is a very thorough piece of work that places considerable emphasis on Bridie's structural skill. Winifred Bannister's *James Bridie and his Theatre* is highly commended as a storehouse of information about dates of first performances, names of directors and players, and the reactions of critics and public to these first performances. Other critical studies referred to are listed in the Select Bibliography.

The texts I have used are those published by Constable either singly or in collections; and for permission to quote from these I should like to thank the publishers. In pursuing this survey of nine major Bridie plays, I have also taken the opportunity to range widely amongst his other works. In particular, for certain biographical details, comments, and quotations, I have found his autobiography *One Way of Living* invaluable.

For helpful advice and encouragement in the early stages of this study I am indebted to Professor John MacQueen of the School of Scottish Studies, Edinburgh University.

J.T.L.

BIOGRAPHICAL NOTE

JAMES BRIDIE was born Osborne Henry Mavor on January 3, 1888, in a residential district of Glasgow called Pollokshields. His father was Henry Mavor, who had had a varied career as clerk in a business firm, seaman on a windjammer, and medical student, before becoming an engineer. For the first five years of his life Bridie lived at East Kilbride six miles south of Glasgow, near the birthplace of the anatomist John Hunter. He was brought up in an atmosphere of books and art. He tells us that his father used to read to his children from the Authorised Version of the Bible and from the works of Carlyle, Shakespeare, Stevenson, Tennyson, Browning, Ruskin, and that he himself was taken to see *Macbeth* "some time after" he had written his first play *King Robert the Bruce.* He writes of having early developed "a literary style" as he calls it, which he thought owed something to Shakespeare whose writings were "the only good influence in my early life to which I did not put up a sturdy and mulish resistance".

Bridie was educated first at the High School of Glasgow and then at the Glasgow Academy—a school attended also by J.M. Barrie, John Reith (later of the BBC), Walter Elliot and D.Y. Cameron the artist. He himself developed an interest and a skill in art: indeed for a time he wanted to be an artist; but, his father having reservations about this, he decided he would be a doctor instead because that meant he would be able to drive about in a brougham! He found school work boring and was not very good at games. The one thing that made him celebrated, or rather notorious, was school journalism: he produced two lithographed magazines called *The Kernel* and *The Tomahawk.*

9

The latter, being original to the point of scurrility, brought upon him the wrath of the Rector.

In 1904, having passed his preliminary examinations in medicine, he entered the University of Glasgow and was introduced by his father to John Cleland, the professor of anatomy. We notice how the anatomy motif recurs in Bridie's life story. He himself in his autobiography stresses his own connection with the historical figure whom he was to portray in his first great doctor play:

> Johnny Cleland had been taught by Goodsir, who had been taught by Knox, who was the patron of Burke and Hare.

Bridie seems to have had a great deal of social life at this time. He enjoyed going to the theatre and appears to have already developed a taste for musical shows and Shakespeare. By the time he had been four years at the University he had become well attuned to the life, taking an active part in rectorial campaigns, becoming celebrated as writer and composer of songs, and eventually serving as editor of Glasgow University Magazine.

In 1913 Bridie became a doctor and joined the staff of the Royal Infirmary as House Physician to W.R. Jack. When war broke out in 1914, he joined the R.A.M.C., and was subsequently sent to France, serving at Ypres and the Somme. After a spell at home on sick light duty, during which time he met Esmé Percy and heard him perform, Bridie was again caught up in the activity of war and sent to Mesopotamia. He has given an account of his war-time experiences in the East in his book *Some Talk of Alexander* (1926). He seems to have enjoyed his experiences in India, Mesopotamia, Persia, and Constantinople; he certainly turned them to good account in the biblical plays he wrote later. *Tobias and the Angel,*

10

Susannah and the Elders, and *Jonah* testify to his interest in these countries as well as to his knowledge of scripture.

Near the end of the war he was involved in fighting the influenza epidemic as it affected North Persia; and a few years later he was engaged in similar work in Britain. These experiences are reflected in the final scenes of *A Sleeping Clergyman* in which Charles Cameron the Second struggles to find a means of halting the pandemic in Britain. When he was released from the army in 1919, Bridie bought a practice in the Langside district of Glasgow and joined the staff of the Victoria Infirmary as a junior assistant physician. His views on medical etiquette and his refusal to reveal anything about his cases link up with the characterisation of Johnson in *Dr. Angelus*; and his sceptical or at least detached attitude towards psychologists and the unconscious is reflected in his treatment of Dr. Pothecary in *The Baikie Charivari.* He seems to have enjoyed his hospital work but was not particularly happy as a general practitioner. Although he could not have had a great deal of time, he managed to write a fair amount without earning very much. The first draft of his first full-length play *The Switchback* failed to impress Alfred Wareing of the Glasgow Repertory Theatre and was pushed into a drawer.

In 1923 Bridie sold his practice and became an assistant physician at Victoria Infirmary. Shortly afterwards he was appointed professor at the Anderson College of Medicine. This was the year of his marriage to Rona Locke Bremner; and although he had very little money behind him, he felt a great welling up of confidence within him at this time. In the course of the next few years he became more and more involved in the theatre. He renewed acquaintance with Dr. John MacIntyre now John Brandane dramatist and chief supporter of the Scottish National Theatre Society. This society had just engaged a young professional producer called Tyrone Guthrie when Bridie was asked by Brandane to join the board. It was also about this time that he wrote a play called *The Sunlight Sonata*, which was revised and trimmed according to advice by Guthrie and Brandane, and presented at the Lyric Theatre, Glasgow, in March 1928. In response to Brandane's request for a full-length play, Bridie pulled *The Switchback* out of the drawer where it had lain for five years and subjected it to Brandane's criticism and tailoring. It was accepted by Barry Jackson for production at the Birmingham Repertory Theatre in the spring of 1929.

The next important event for Bridie was the production at Birmingham in the same year of a second play *What it is to be Young;* but even more important was the request from the Masque Theatre in Glasgow for a play about Burke and Hare which led to the writing of *The Anatomist* and its production in Edinburgh in the summer of 1930. In the same year *Tobias and the Angel* was written and sent to Tyrone Guthrie, who, with Amner Hall, was working at the Cambridge Festival Theatre. This play was produced by Evan John at Cambridge with Tyrone Guthrie as the Archangel. Bridie was now well on the way towards being an established dramatist. His first London production came in 1932 when *The Anatomist* was produced at the Westminster, directed by Tyrone Guthrie and starring Henry Ainley and Flora Robson.

A landmark was reached with the writing and production of *A Sleeping Clergyman* in 1933. Bridie himself, although critical of it, thought it one of his more important plays; the Malvern audience were greatly impressed; and there was one performance in Glasgow that so held the audience as to convince people that here was something exceptional. From this time up to 1939 a steady stream of plays came from Bridie's pen, including *Marriage is no*

Joke and *Colonel Wotherspoon* (1934), slight pieces not very successful in production, *Mary Read* (1934) and *The Black Eye* (1935) both reasonably successful when first produced, more serious plays like *Babes in the Wood* and *The King of Nowhere* (1938)—the first featuring a schoolmaster as Faust figure and the second a megalomaniac Scottish politician, another biblical play *Susannah and the Elders* (1937), and a Scottish play which deals with the conflict between the outsider and the unco guid *The Golden Legend of Shults* (1939).

In 1939 Bridie rejoined the R.A.M.C. as Major, after being awarded a Doctor of Laws degree by Glasgow University. In 1942 he was asked to become a member of the Council for the Encouragement of Music and the Arts, and was appointed Chairman of the Scottish Committee. He seemed to be dividing his writing time between biblical plays or romances and Scottish plays. *Jonah 3* was performed at Manchester in 1942 and *Holy Isle* in the same year at the Arts Theatre, London. *Lancelot* was produced at the Royal Princess's Theatre by the Citizens' Company in 1945. The two great Scottish plays of the war years were *Mr. Bolfry*, produced in London in 1943, and *The Forrigan Reel,* produced at the Athenaeum by the Citizens' in 1944.

The Glasgow Citizens' Theatre had been founded in 1943 with Bridie as Chairman of the Board; and in 1945 the Citizens' Company took over and settled in their permanent home—the Royal Princess's Theatre which had been offered to them on a ten years' lease. A year or so later Bridie was actively involved in helping to establish the Edinburgh International Festival. With Robert Kemp, Tyrone Guthrie and others he was responsible for negotiating for the use of the Assembly Hall for the first production of a Scottish play at the heart of the official festival. The Kemp-Guthrie revival of *The Thrie Estaitis*,

David Lyndsay's mediaeval Morality play, proved one of the greatest successes in recent Scottish dramatic history: it was performed at the festival four times after its initial production in 1948. Even although he must have been immensely busy during these five years after the Second World War, serving on boards, organising productions for the Citizens' and for the Festival, he found time to write more plays. *Dr. Angelus* was first performed in Edinburgh and London in 1947; *Gog and Magog*, based on the life of McGonagall the Dundee doggerel poet, was first performed at the Arts Theatre, London, in 1948; and his first full experiment in symbolist drama *Daphne Laureola* was first given at Wyndham's in 1949, produced by Laurence Olivier and starring Edith Evans. In 1950, amidst all his activities, Bridie founded the first school of drama in Scotland—the College of Drama of the Royal Scottish Academy of Music.

Between 1949 and 1950 Bridie was writing his last plays—*Mr. Gillie*, first produced in 1950 by the Citizens' and later presented at the Garrick Theatre, London, *The Queen's Comedy,* first performed at the Edinburgh Festival in 1950 by the Citizens' and directed by Tyrone Guthrie, and *The Baikie Charivari*, first performed posthumously in 1952 at the Citizens'. It seems that the year 1950 was the great climax and time of fulfilment for Bridie: he was experimenting with different forms of drama and he at last achieved a production of one of his own plays at the Edinburgh International Festival. But he must have been sorely overtaxing his powers. At the beginning of 1951 his physical condition worsened; and on January 29, 1951, he died in the Edinburgh Royal Infirmary of a vascular condition.

James Bridie, Osborne Henry Mavor, emerges from the pages of biography as a rather shy Puckish figure, frequently posing as lazy and unsociable, but in reality a

14

man of dynamic powers and immense intellectual energy. His medical knowledge and experience informed many of his plays; and his questing nature, his idealism, and his belief in art and the artist are reflected throughout his writings. The undergraduate in him relished debunking and supplied the fun, the pantomime and the humour; the mature man presented his characters, themes and social problems from an intellectual viewpoint essentially Scottish in its delight in argument and philosophical discussion. It was typical of Bridie that he should die in the full flush of all his activities—literary, theatrical, administrative. He would have been the first to admit his indebtedness to others—to his father, to John Brandane, to Tyrone Guthrie, and to many others—actors, dramatists, public figures. On the other hand his life story reveals how much he himself did for drama and the artistic life of Scotland. Many people who have been stimulated and impressed by his works have felt the need for a critical re-appraisal of his contribution to dramatic literature. The study of nine of his more important plays that follows is an attempt to help in that re-appraisal.

CHAPTER ONE

THREE DOCTOR MORALITY PLAYS

IT IS APPROPRIATE to begin with a consideration of three of Bridie's doctor plays, because Bridie perhaps more than any other modern playwright has studied the medical mind at work and given it vivid presentation on the stage.

It appears he was rather critical of Shaw's *The Doctor's Dilemma* (1906). Winifred Bannister tells us that he spoke snappishly of "those ridiculous phagocytes". Nevertheless, there are obvious links between this play of Shaw's in which the fashionable doctor is satirised and Bridie's first doctor play *The Switchback* where the idealism of the young Dr. Mallaby is set against the hypocrisy of the prosperous surgeon Sir Anthony Craye. In *The Switchback* one can discern the characteristic Bridie technique—the concentrating on the figure of a medical man with a purpose (Mallaby seeks a cure for phthisis) and the highlighting of that purpose in moral terms. The problem becomes more complicated when Bridie comes to deal with figures who are actors or poseurs as well as doctors—Knox in *The Anatomist,* Angelus in *Dr. Angelus:* the moral aspect is either blurred or turned inside out. In *The Switchback* and in *Dr. Angelus* we find straightforward studies of the young medical idealist— Mallaby, Johnson; but the most positive moral statement, the notion that genius has to be nurtured for the good of mankind, is to be found in neither of these but in *A Sleeping Clergyman.*

I have called Bridie's three major doctor plays Doctor Morality Plays because they present facets of good and evil in medical life, and because, as in the old Morality plays, good triumphs over evil in the end. The doctors in these plays are not all evil angels: some are good, some are bad; and one is generally a kind of medical Everyman—sinning, seeking salvation, looking for a medical Holy Grail.

The Anatomist (1930) is based on certain incidents in the life of the nineteenth-century Edinburgh anatomist Dr. Robert Knox. Knox was implicated in the body-snatching activities of the resurrectionists and the West Port murders committed by the Irishmen William Burke and William Hare between 1828 and 1829. In his author's note to the play, Bridie describes the impressions of Knox that emerge from history and Lonsdale's biography. The theatricality of the man, his intellectual qualities, his rhetorical style of speaking and harsh pleasantries, his love of fine clothes—these are characteristics that seem to have caught Bridie's interest. He was attracted also by the melodramatic possibilities of the Burke and Hare story and the tragical potential of the incident on which the Mary Paterson murder is founded.

The Anatomist could be called a historical drama or melodrama. It presents to begin with a dramatisation of events taken from early nineteenth-century history—the history of the resurrectionists, people like Burke and Hare who were prepared to commit murder to provide bodies for the anatomists. It represents the actions and character of a historical personage—the dynamic Dr. Knox. It is also a human study of people caught in a tangle of emotions—Walter Anderson and Mary Belle, Dr. Knox and Amelia, Mary Paterson and her "black" life, Davie Paterson and his pretensions. It may be said also to have a third level, a kind of mythological plane on which we see the archetypal seeker after truth, a kind of medical Everyman, beset by evils and committing evil, guilty of *hubris*, but reaching some state of grace whereby he gains insight and is given strength to continue his pursuit of the Holy Grail.

Structurally, the play is simple and yet striking in its balance and tone contrasts. The first and third acts, set in the Disharts' drawing-room, may be described as basically social and disquisitory in tone. The atmosphere at the beginning of each of these acts is essentially domestic; indeed there is at the beginning of the first act something of the exaggerated bourgeois tone of comfort that recalls the atmosphere of Barrie's *Quality Street*. But both these acts have their domesticity broken—by disquisition or by an upsetting personality or event. The chief topic of discussion arises from the conflict between love and the demands of medical research; domestic calm is disturbed by the dynamic personality of the anatomist himself. The second act, which is divided into two scenes the one set in a tavern the other in a mortuary, is melodramatic and romantic in the sense of being highly coloured and emotional. In this middle movement, the setting of the tavern with its intrigue, its drunkenness and loose living, and the atmosphere of the mortuary, heightened by Walter's emotional outbursts, are in vivid contrast to the respectability and bourgeois background of the first and third movements.

Knox is the centre point of the play. Our conception of his character and the actor's interpretation of the part may well help us to work out and understand one of the great themes of the play. Of the two contrasting interpretations of the part—Henry Ainley's and Alastair Sim's, Bridie himself seemed to prefer the Ainley interpretation: he once said that the part should be played in the style of a "barnstorming tenor". Yet in Act III he makes Amelia say to Knox "Now try to be a man and not a barnstorming tenor". It appears that Ainley's interpretation stressed the swashbuckling melodramatic aspects in an attractive, perhaps superficial manner, whereas Sim paid more attention to Knox's concern for medical progress, his crusade for anatomical enlightenment, and his significant realisation of the sins he committed while pursuing his aims:

> . . . Do you think because I strut and rant and put on a bold face that my soul isn't sick within me at the horror of what I have done? What *I* have done . . . No, I carry the deaths of these poor wretches round my neck till I die. (Act III)

This second interpretation seems to me to pinpoint the high theme of the play—the conflict between the pursuit of medical progress and the doubtful means used to achieve that progress. Knox may appear on the surface to be the ranting barnstormer; but in the course of the play he undergoes a process of integration partly because of his experiences and partly because of Amelia's influence, so that by the end he realises the price he has to pay for his medical knowledge. His dilemma is similar to that of Faustus:

> But I tell you this, that the cause is between Robert Knox and Almighty God. (Act III)

This summarises the conflict that is at the heart of the play and illustrates its strong Morality element. It also illustrates a Scottish quality—a concern with religion and an insistence on dealing with God direct. Along with this goes another Scottish trait—the pursuing of an interest or study with great moral intensity. Mary Belle gives a rather distorted view of Knox's obsession with his medical work:

> I think you are a vain, hysterical, talented, stupid man. I think that you are wickedly blind and careless when your mind is fixed on something . . . (Act III)

The play as a whole, as it builds up to its final climaxes, gives a clearer view of this high theme and its Scottish quality. As Helen L. Luyben puts it, Knox has "rationally chosen to carry the deaths of poor wretches around his neck until he dies because he believes it is his duty to pass along the knowledge he has acquired".

The other characters contribute to the leading motifs of the play by throwing against them distortions, contrasts, or parodies. Walter Anderson echoes Knox's passion for medical research in bursts that become fainter as the play goes on; his enthusiasm for anatomy lacks Knox's moral drive and dissolves finally into sentimentality and conventional attitudes. Davie Paterson, the janitor at Surgeons' Hall, is, like Knox, concerned with religion, but he sounds the religious motif in a parodied form. His is the mealy-mouthed hypocritical attitude to religion and the Bible in contrast to Knox's poetic and morally dynamic attitude. Mary Belle and Amelia add their own counter-pointing to the high Knoxian theme. Amelia, aware of Knox's genius, yet contrives to "earth" it by opposing to his rhetorical outbursts her own humanity and practical wisdom. Mary Belle's counterpoint is the sharpest and is as much a commentary on her own prim conventional little mind as on Knox's pomposity. As we have noted, she presents the theme of Knox's single-minded pursuit of anatomy in such a way as to distort it and reveal the distortions she thinks she traces within its rhythms. Mary Paterson may be considered, in Mrs Bannister's words, as merely "a harlot of harsh voice and vulgar maudlin speech", but it is clear there is a strong element of tragedy in the part—a quality that was brought out by Flora Robson in the 1931 production. There are at least two touches in the script that vividly and significantly illustrate the tragic potential. The first is Mary's tenderness and concern for Walter Anderson (and Walter's sympathetic reaction); the second is the song she sings with its combination of sweetness and bitterness:

Can ye sew cushions and can ye sew sheets,
And can ye sing Balaloo
When the bairnie greets? . . .

Black's the life I lead wi' the hale o' ye—(Act II, Scene I)

This, when viewed in the context of her death at the hands of Burke and Hare, adds a dimension that illustrates the human pathos, the suffering and the tragedy that are concomitants of Knox's pursuit of medical knowledge.

Burke and Hare are not used merely as necessary historical background material. Certainly they contribute powerfully to the atmosphere of villainy and melodrama in the middle part of the play; but they are also closely woven into its thematic texture. They provide bodies for the anatomists so that the work of medical science may progress; and in their own way they too are concerned about religion: after delivering the corpse in Act II Scene II, they are anxious not to be late for early Mass. In other words they serve medical science and fear God in their way as Knox does in his.

In the end the focus of critical attention must return to the figure of Robert Knox himself. As we have indicated, he embodies the main theme of the play; so that it is possible to regard him in one way as a villain in that he uses or connives at foul means of obtaining corpses, and in another as a martyr in that he is threatened and denounced by the public while making a great contribution to medical progress. It seems that James Agate and other reviewers were critical of Bridie for not writing a final act that would have presented Knox as villain or martyr. Presumably it was felt that the ending was ambiguous in the sense that there is no conclusive *coup de théâtre*. In fact, what Bridie did do was something much more subtle, logical and penetrating. The last scene depicting Knox resuming his work for humanity while being assailed by the forces of ignorance, far from being an anti-climax, illustrates a positive aspect of the major theme of the play. Bridie provided alternative endings to the final speech. In the first Knox begins a lecture on the heart of the rhinoceros; in the second he begins a lecture on the human heart. The rhinoceros ending throws emphasis on Knox's own super-human energy; the other throws the emphasis on his humanity. Either way we have an illustration of the high courage of the man in pursuing his medical work in the teeth of opposition representing ignorance and perhaps also the forces of evil he himself had harnessed. The ending as a whole is not only dignified and dramatic: it is structurally and psychologically sound and artistic. At the beginning Knox has spoken in a swashbuckling manner of his desire to have a chance to face the mob with his back to the wall and pistols in his hand; at the end he is menaced by the mob but instead of violence offers something more positive—the continuation of his work for medical science in the form of a lecture to his students. He is neither martyr nor villain but has reached a state of wisdom, if not grace, as a result of his experiences and suffering, and perhaps also as a result of his confession to Amelia of the wrongs he had caused in pursuing his studies.

The ending of the play has strength too in its mythic and universal planes. In Knox's description of the rhinoceros's heart we have an impression of the tremendous energy that exists in the world and a reminder of his own; in his description of the human heart we are reminded of what has provided the motive power for the conflicts and the aspirations depicted in the play. Finally, in his return to his real work—the pursuit of medical knowledge—we have a last view of the Knoxian search for the Holy Grail.

The writing of *A Sleeping Clergyman* (1933) appears to have caused Bridie a great deal of trouble. He was engaged on it for the best part of two years and seems at times to have been in despair about it. It was on themes that fascinated him—eugenics, heredity, medical research, a cure for a scourge of a disease; but the shaping and structuring of episodes which spanned a period of sixty years raised problems for a dramatist who had been strongly influenced by the conventions of the naturalistic three-act play. *A Sleeping Clergyman* is in fact a two-act play, each part owing something to a historical event or historical background.

The story of Madeleine Smith, the Glasgow woman who was tried for the murder of her lover Emile L'Angelier in 1857 and released on a "not proven" verdict, seems to have had an attraction for writers of the late nineteenth and early twentieth centuries. Many books and some plays were written on the subject. Some aspects of the story are woven into the first part of *A Sleeping Clergyman* in the episode where Wilhelmina poisons John Hannah. Hannah, like Emile L'Angelier, was inferior to his lover socially, but could on occasion, also like L'Angelier, be arrogant and dictatorial. Wilhelmina, like Madeleine, was a passionate woman out to satisfy her sexual desires, and, also like Madeleine, she wrote wildly passionate love letters with which the man was able later to blackmail her. Poisoning the lover seemed the natural way out for the woman when she saw the need for a more respectable match.

In writing the second part of the play, Bridie must have been influenced also by his experiences as a doctor during the influenza epidemic that swept Britain and the Continent just after the First World War. The main themes running through the play and emphasised in its second part—eugenics, heredity, the preservation of genius, the search for a cure for an infectious disease— were subjects much debated by medical people, writers, and intelligent laymen in the early part of the twentieth century. George Bernard Shaw had dealt with similar themes in works like *Man and Superman* (1903), *The Doctor's Dilemma* (1906), *Back to Methuselah* (1921); and Aldous Huxley painted a grimmer picture of the possibilities of selective breeding in his novel *Brave New World* (1932).

Structurally, historically, and thematically, then, *A Sleeping Clergyman* is a very important Bridie play, even if it is not held in high esteem by all critics. Bridie himself felt its importance. In *One Way of Living* he wrote: "As this curious play was the nearest thing to a masterpiece I shall probably write, perhaps you will allow me to spend a little time on it". But he was aware of its weaknesses too— particularly in the second part. He added in that same self-critical note: "It was not a masterpiece. The second act attempted an impossibility and failed badly". Winifred Bannister had great praise for the play, particularly for its dramatic power, its dialogue, and its characterisation, but she was critical of its architecture. Helen L. Luyben thought *A Sleeping Clergyman* a much less subtle (and therefore less satisfactory) play than *Tobias and the Angel*. She appeared to be critical of Bridie for dropping his

24

judicial attitude and for making it clear that good had triumphed in the end. Gabriel Marcel in his essay "Le Théâtre de James Bridie" admitted that the play was not to his taste, and he cited as his reasons its melodramatic realism, its naiveté, its lack of subtlety. He was not impressed with the importance of the theme either. Writing in 1957, he felt that this kind of drama was out of date— "étrangement loin de ce qui nous requiert ou nous touche aujourd' hui". Ursula Gerber in *James Bridies Dramen* appreciated the skilful shaping of dialogue and dramatic tension but she complained of the absence of an ordinary human atmosphere in the play: ". . . vermissen wir den schlichten, echt menschlichen Ton".

The points of criticism raised by Helen Luyben and Gabriel Marcel direct our attention to the movement of the play towards an explicit conclusion and resolution. It is true that Bridie demonstrates dramatically the triumph of the good over the evil, the evolution of Charles Cameron the Second as a great healer, the success of his cure for the pandemic. *A Sleeping Clergyman* is a kind of medical Morality; but from time to time it becomes unfashionable in literary circles to be moral or optimistic and to hope for positive results from the advance of science. On the other hand, it is important to observe that the ending of the play is by no means wholly optimistic: Hope expresses her fears of over-population, and even old Marshall wonders if the world is worth the tremendous efforts made by Cameron. Ursula Gerber's stricture on the lack of humanity in the play does remind us too that the main character is an abstraction or a number of abstractions like heredity, genius, the preservation of the gene, and not a person or personality.

If these criticisms were entirely valid, however, one would expect that the play would have proved a failure in production. In fact, this was not the case, despite the difficulties of staging its eleven scenes. At the first performance at the Malvern Festival in 1933, it had an enthusiastic reception; and later at the Piccadilly Theatre, London, it ran for 230 performances. It was also well received by Scottish audiences—particularly in Glasgow. When it was revived in 1947 by the Glasgow Citizens' Theatre, it again proved popular with the general public and the critics. What it needs is regular revival so that each age may have a chance to pass judgment on its relevance and dramatic effectiveness.

There can be no doubt that *A Sleeping Clergyman* has considerable dramatic power and brilliant dialogue. These qualities are illustrated in the first part in particular where the Charles Cameron-Harriet confrontation is skilfully handled and the John Hannah-Wilhelmina melodrama effectively presented. There has however been criticism of some of its features—its use of a chorus, its episodic technique. Some early critics could not see the point of the figure of the sleeping clergyman himself; others thought that Dr. Marshall was not necessary to the development of the plot; above all the play was criticised for its sprawling nature, for these eleven different scenes that are so difficult to stage smoothly. What we have to remember, however, is that *A Sleeping Clergyman* is unified by its own high themes which by being illustrated through different characters provide the centrality normally provided by one or two main figures. Also, we have to see it as an experiment with time controlled by the device of the chorus. In other words we should try to view this piece, not as a conventional social-realist drama, but more in the tradition of Greek practice in its use of chorus and its fusing of time past and time present, more in the tradition of the Morality play in dealing with the evil and the good within the same individual, more in the tradition of Shakespearean drama in its use of a series of scenes in which the theme

26

emerges from a variety of settings and angles.

The play is divided into two parts, each introduced by a chorus (the two doctors Cooper and Coutts) and each subdivided into scenes—four in the first and five in the second. Thus there seems justification for the criticism that it is episodic in structure, except that there are these unifying devices—the chorus with its sleeping clergyman (Bridie's "enigmatic . . . distant and impersonal" God, as Helen Luyben describes him), Dr. William Marshall (God's deputy, keeping the spark of genius alive), and the hereditary or creative urge as central character. There is also, as we have already noted, something of the technique of Greek drama about the play: it features a chorus, it fuses different time periods, and it builds up a structure of ideas rather than scenes or characters. Indeed, in the unfolding of a chain of tragic horror-events broken at last by the power of positive good—the discovery of a cure for the pandemic, *A Sleeping Clergyman* resembles the *Oresteia* of Aeschylus.

What bedevilled Bridie in the writing of *A Sleeping Clergyman* was a feeling that he had to subscribe to realism in setting and situation most of the time. The paradox is that when he is constructing his parable or romance (the salvation of the world by someone emerging from squalor and obscurity) his play is at its most dramatic when he is not being realist at all. The most exciting episodes are in the form of melodrama in Part One; the most stimulating parts are in the form of argument and discussion—mostly in Part Two. The unifying character *is* an idea; the banalities of colloquial speech are used to throw into high relief the more artificial style of the vital arguments and key speeches. Although he himself may not have been fully aware of it, Bridie constructed *A Sleeping Clergyman,* with its multiplicity of scenes, more in the manner of a film, a Greek play, a Shakespeare drama. Clearly it is best suited to an unlocalised stage, although the author himself sketched realist settings for each scene. Winifred Bannister believed the failure of the New York production by the Theatre Guild of New York in 1934 was due to the use of nine naturalistic scenes (in accordance with Bridie's own stage directions). It is inevitable that the rhythms of the play should be destroyed by such frequent delays for scene shifting. On the other hand, the great success of the original Malvern production of 1933 may well have been due to Paul Shelving's simple staging. His plain setting of backcloth and wings must have given the director the flexibility so essential to the rapid unfolding of the scenes. It seems to me that the structure of the play as written is sufficiently firm to bear an unbroken development in production. If the play were presented swiftly in the open style of Shakespearean productions by Poel, Granville Barker and Tyrone Guthrie, on an uncluttered stage, we would be less aware of any architectural weaknesses and more aware of its steadily developing themes and the power of its moments of insight and high drama.

Of its intellectual qualities there seems to have been no doubt from the start. The most discerning of the early reviewers were clearly aware of its argumentative force and the provocative treatment of its themes. The critic of *The Observer* of the day noticed that the discussion on eugenics had "something of the serious force of a good Scottish sermon". This may remind us of the influence of Shaw again; but in fact the intensity with which the moral and intellectual problems are handled in the debates between Charles Cameron the First and Dr. Marshall and in the discussions between Charles Cameron the Second, the Walkers, and Hope, seems to me characteristically Scottish. It is possible to regard the feature that Helen Luyben objects to—the clear triumph of good over evil—

28

as a basically Scottish one, owing its unequivocal nature to Bridie's Presbyterian upbringing. Nor is the picture of squalor and sordidness unrelated to the Scottish scene or mind: the two sides of the Scottish character—the idealistic and the squalid, the puritanical and the debauched—are presented as clearly in *A Sleeping Clergyman* as they are in Burns's *Holy Willie's Prayer*, Hogg's *The Private Memoirs and Confessions of a Justified Sinner*, and Robert Louis Stevenson's *Dr. Jekyll and Mr Hyde*.

Does *A Sleeping Clergyman* lack the human quality, as Ursula Gerber suggests? It is true that Bridie is more concerned with showing the triumph of a medical ideal than with the study of a human character. But a play that contains such a scene as that between Charles Cameron the First and Marshall, with its impression of a strong human relationship, or that between Cameron and Harriet, with its sharply caught man-woman conflict, can hardly be said to lack human qualities. Perhaps in the second part there is too much concern for the working out of the cure; but even here one finds considerable power in the characterisation of Charles Cameron the Second and his sister Hope, and in the caricatures of the Walkers. Bridie has in fact given us not one or two studies of humanity but five or six or more. The leading players have the chance to switch rôles as in Greek drama. The leading man has two Cameron characters to act—both dissolute but the one sinking into his squalor and the other rising out of it. The leading lady has the opportunity to present three studies— Harriet, Wilhelmina, Hope—all well observed, three-dimensional characters. Harriet is the Scottish bourgeoise who plays with sex but wants all to be made respectable; Wilhelmina is the experimenter in sex, passionate and mocking, whose nemesis is inevitable. Hope is the cool intellectual version, satirical and far-seeing, with more than a hint of humanity underneath. Amongst the others are two typically Scottish figures—John Hannah and his mother. Hannah is the dour Scot of working-class origin, intensely keen to pursue his studies, a hypocrite posing as a puritan, with the fires of ambition and sensualism smouldering underneath. Mrs Hannah is the Scottish housewife, the landlady of shrewish voice keeping her lodgers in order and hiding her maternal qualities under a hard exterior. The Walkers are typical Anglo-Scots—affected, ambitious, snobbish: they are the ideal foil for the Camerons. Marshall, like the Duke in *Measure for Measure,* has a dual function: he is a character in his own right, a kindly conventional but wise doctor; and he is also the representative of God, the preserver of the gene, and ultimately the prophet of the Cameron heredity.

At the end of the play the focus sharpens on him: it is he who in a moving and illuminating way uses the *nunc dimittis* quotation: "Now lettest thou thy servant depart in peace"; and it is from his mouth that we hear the final chords of the great heredity theme of the whole play:

> I did my best to keep the spark alive, and now it's a great flame in Charlie and in you. Humanity will warm its hands at you.

A suggestion of doubt about the value of serving mankind returns us to a more objective note at the end. Marshall knows that Charlie has it in him to "do great things for the world ... if the world is worth it". Hope for once seems to see farther than the old man: "Whether the world is worth it or not". The ending thus links structure and technique with the high theme of the play. The driving force of genius and heredity which we have seen personified and dramatised in the Charles Camerons could be *saeva Necessitas* after all, or the workings of that "enigmatic ... impersonal" deity—the Sleeping Clergyman himself.

Dr. Angelus (1947) is based on the case of Dr. Pritchard, the Glasgow doctor who, in 1865, was found guilty of murdering his mother-in-law and his wife by poisoning. Bridie seems to have absorbed his source material thoroughly here. Pritchard posed as a man of religion and an affectionate husband; before his main crimes committed in Sauchiehall Street he was suspected of being implicated in a fire in a previous house in Berkeley Terrace in which a young servant girl lost her life; and at the time of the poisoning he was carrying on a sordid affair with another servant girl Mary McLeod. These features of the legal case are reproduced in the play; and the name of the mother-in-law—Mrs Taylor—is common to both.

Dr. Angelus has some of the qualities of a *roman policier;* and Bridie makes of it a *pièce noire* that at a first impression would appear to emphasise the seamy side of life—murder by poisoning, adultery, deceptions, acts of gross hypocrisy. The figure of Angelus dominates the play, as the figure of Knox dominates *The Anatomist:* there is an aura of evil about both men; but whereas Knox is dedicated to medical science, Angelus is dedicated to his own self-gratification, recalling the evil genius of Jonson's Volpone, the hypocrisy of Angelo in *Measure for Measure*, and the arrogance of Marlowe's Faustus.

This play has many of the ingredients required for an immediate success on the stage—a strongly drawn central character, tense moments of melodrama, and a fair modicum of wit and humour; and these qualities no doubt accounted for the warm reception it received in June 1947 in Edinburgh and in July of the same year at the Phoenix Theatre, London, where it ran for seven months. This popularity contrasts oddly with the complicated reactions and objections of some early critics. Sewell Stokes in his essay "The English Spotlight" (1947) was unsure whether or not to take Bridie's villain seriously, and wondered if perhaps he was deliberately confusing us as to the kind of play he was writing. Hunter Diack in an article in *The Spectator,* August 1947, made the suggestion that Angelus' mind so dominates the play that "we take sides with his larger lunacy against the callow or moronic creatures who people the ordinary world". It is possible that the oscillation of the character of Angelus between fantasy and realism may tend to confuse those who have fixed ideas about *genres* in dramatic writings; and it is possible that if we allowed ourselves to be immersed in Angelus' talk and philosophising we might begin to share Diack's viewpoint. But I think this is to complicate the matter unnecessarily. Perhaps the early audiences seeing the play as theatrical entertainment were right after all. The shape and structure as apparent on the stage bring out the hypocrisy of the man and the grim humour of his rôle-playing—features to be traced in the character of the original.

Although Diack's idea that we take sides with Angelus is at first sight attractive, it cannot be supported by an examination of the dramatic structure of the play. The theatricality of Angelus' personality, the risibility of his cliché-ridden language, and the melodramas he stages all tend to distance him as a character; and, thrown up in high relief against his partner Dr. Johnson and *his* transparent honesty, he becomes a force for evil, a sham, a self-centred monster. It is significant that those points at which the play moves away from external action towards theorising or fantasy or philosophical discussion are precisely the places where we have a moral code set up as a contrast to the immoral intrigue that is being unfolded. Systematic poisoning and deception are central to the dramatic action of the play: these are the leitmotifs that run through the action; but these are constantly being thrown against the positive values—the loyalty, honesty and idealism of young Dr. Johnson who is deceived by Angelus and persuaded to sign the death certificates. In Johnson's first dialogue with Mrs Corcoran in Act One the references to the Holy Grail and the reciting of the Hippocratic Oath are closely built in to the moral structure of the play. Against this may be set Angelus' "hypothetical" statement in Act Three about the man hemmed in by domestic tyranny and determined to go to any lengths to break loose and express himself—a statement made the more diabolical for being spoken over the recumbent figure of Johnson himself.

Helen Luyben believes that the play is a bitter judgment of man, and Hunter Diack believes that the characters of the ordinary world appear callow or moronic alongside Angelus. My own impression is that the structure and technique of the third act illustrate the shallowness rather than the depth of Angelus and the strength rather than the weakness of Johnson. As for Inspector MacIvor, far from being moronic, he seems to me to bring the calm light of reason and a sense of justice that make their own comment on the strange case of the diabolic Dr. Angelus and the altruistic Dr. Johnson. For the play, it seems to me, is essentially a Morality with strong Scottish overtones that suggest the two sides to man's moral nature. The case of Dr. Angelus and Dr. Johnson, even if it is entirely different from that of Dr. Jekyll and Mr Hyde in plot, treatment and style, has at its heart something of the same sharp contrast between the good and the evil, the upright and the warped.

The two doctors are the main characters, both apparently devoted to their calling. Johnson is the young doctor of great promise, anxious to become immersed in the work of healing the sick, and flattered at being treated as an equal by the experienced Dr. Angelus. The resistance he puts up to Mrs Corcoran's advances and his reciting the

Hippocratic Oath illustrate his high standards and idealism; his medical discussions with Angelus and Butt show his developing skill as a doctor; and the deep psychological disturbances he suffers, symbolised by the dream-fantasy, illustrate his moral sensitivity. If we pay insufficient attention to the part played by Johnson and its significance for the whole play, we are in danger of misunderstanding its moral structure. No doubt Angelus tends to dominate; and no doubt he seems at times to dazzle and bewilder his young partner. What we have in effect is an exaggerated portrait of an evil doctor at the heart of this apparently naturalistic play. The mixture of exaggeration and realism works as an effective pattern on the stage; and the play is at its most impressive precisely in those sequences that are essentially non-realistic—in the theorisings, the monologues, the fantasy. These sequences, allied to the sharp moral contrast between the two figures, point to an allegorical purpose: behind the contrasted characterisations lies the truth of the moral statement.

The other characters are more important for the parts they play in the total design than for any memorable qualities. They are supporters of the evil or the good— Jeanie, Mrs Corcoran; or they comment on the nature of Angelus' evil actions—Mrs Angelus, Sir Gregory Butt, Inspector MacIvor. It is true that incidentally we have impressions of a sluttish servant lassie, a discontented but well-meaning young married woman, a weakened brow-beaten wife, a pompous self-regarding medical specialist, a shrewd but humane police inspector; but whether these characterisations are fully developed or not is irrelevant: they have to fit into the pattern of the whole play as members of Bridie's chorus rather than individually in a portrait gallery.

Dr. Angelus is, on the surface, a naturalistic play set in a doctor's consulting room and divided into three almost

34

equal acts; but is has classical qualities and subtleties achieved by certain devices—monologues that intensify the drama, the use of some characters as chorus figures, and frequent modulation from naturalism to melodrama and fantasy. Within this apparently straightforward play with its one setting throughout, we find in actual fact a variety of linguistic styles, a set of contrasting moods, and dramatic devices used to deepen or broaden the background and scope of the play. The range in language extends from Angelus' fulsome outbursts to Johnson's nervous colloquial style, from Jeanie's Glasgow Scots to Angelus' medical style, from Butt's pompous tones to MacIvor's brisk objectivity. In several passages—particularly in the dream-fantasy—the sharp laconic style of legal cross-examination speeds up the pace. The moods vary from Angelus' assumption of the sententious hard-working doctor-*persona* to his bursts of anger and suspicion at Jeanie or Johnson, from Johnson's moments of idealism to his more objective moments when he is concerned with purely medical matters, from moments of fantasy in which the realities of the intrigue are most obvious, to the moments of matter-of-fact police routine handled by MacIvor. The devices used by Bridie to extend the range of the play are the equivalent of Shakespeare's soliloquies and heightened poetic passages. There is the simple monologue which may contain a straightforward moral statement like the recitation of the Hippocratic Oath or a monologue which may throw one set of moral values against another for ironical contrast as in Angelus' interpretation of Bacon's Idols. There is Johnson's dream-fantasy itself, used to explore his sub-conscious, correct his surface credulity, and point the evil lurking within the façade. In this scene the portrait of Mrs. Taylor's grand-uncle comes to life as a nineteenth-century barrister, and we see Johnson in the witness-box, his back to the

35

audience. As the cross-examination warms up and the lighting strengthens we pick out Angelus in the dock. The briskness of the cross-examination contrasts with the theatricality of the scene; and the facts elicited are precisely those that are preying on Johnson's mind—his doubts, his signing of the death certificate, his suspicions about Mrs. Angelus' illness.

The soliloquy spoken by Angelus over Johnson's unconscious figure is another example of Bridie's varying the technique for an important thematic effect. Here the explanation for the crimes is given out not as a confession but as a kind of ironical hypothesis apparently distant from, though in reality closely bound up with the action. In a series of suppositions Angelus here presents a grandiose and distorted picture of his own frustrations—and thereby an explanation of his crimes:

> Suppose him to be subjected to the incessant attempts of two ignorant and narrow-minded women to mould him to their miserable conception of what a right-thinking domestic animal ought to be ... They are forever trying to lower him into that barber's chair where Samson Judge of Israel was shorn of his strength. Suppose this man to have passionate physical longings. Unless they are satisfied he cannot plan, he cannot think, he cannot rise above the earth ...

This inward climax is sharply interrupted by external action—the arrival of the *deus ex machina* in the form of the police inspector MacIvor. This brings about a highly dramatic dénouement—the disintegration of Angelus and his attempted flight. The theatrical façade begins to crumble. MacIvor earths the emotionalism and conducts the dénouement briskly. From Johnson he brings out the facts of the poisoning; from Jeanie he brings out the nature

36

of the relationship with Angelus, remarking to the unobservant doctor:

A sonsy bit yon ... would you say she was three months or four months gone, Doctor?

It is in keeping with the nature and pattern of the play that the high point in the dénouement should be marked by heroics and an emotional outburst that exposes the scared demented creature lurking beneath the Angelus *persona*. In this final confrontation between MacIvor and Angelus we have the last gleams of evil and pathos before Angelus is finally removed. Towards Johnson Angelus is vindictive; and, far from apologising for himself, he displays a kind of Faustian *hubris*:

Do you think I value my life as little as that, I who have been given this heart and these lungs and this brain to act according to the dictates of my intelligence?

But the practicality of MacIvor brings the argument down to matters of insurance and hanging, with a reference to the wee room in H.M. prison in Duke Street "where better men ... have shaken hands with their lives for the last time". It is this talk of the imminence of Anglus' own death that brings on the emotional outburst; and we are given the full treatment in Angelus' typically melodramatic style, in his wild invocation to "Margaret in heaven", to angels, and to "Jesus tender Shepherd".

It is left to MacIvor as the manipulating figure to comment objectively on Angelus and deal mercifully with Johnson. Johnson's insistence on his own guilt is repentance enough: MacIvor's humane treatment amounts to a sane and balanced judgment. His justice is tempered with commonsense, mercy, and an understanding of the part the young doctor has been obliged to play:

> You'll have a statement to make. See that it is a sensible statement.

The ending of this realist-melodramatic play thus stresses its Morality qualities. Angelus the evil angel has been exposed, and Dr. Johnson as Everyman, in his pursuit of the good, has repented his sins and been judged mercifully.

The dramatic power of these three plays comes from the contrast between the conventional mind and the original mind, the contrast between Mary Belle Dishart and Dr. Knox, between the snobbish Walkers and the dynamic Camerons, between the altruistic Johnson and the diabolical Angelus. Frequently it is a startling illustration of the evil or seamy side of life that heightens the drama—the scenes in the Three Tuns and in the mortuary in *The Anatomist,* the scenes of the Camerons' debauchery in *A Sleeping Clergyman,* the scenes of intrigue between Angelus and Jeanie in *Dr. Angelus.*

Although we cannot claim that these plays are constructed according to strict classical theories or conventions, yet there are aspects of their technique and structure that link them with classical, mediaeval and Elizabethan drama. The tragi-comic structure of *The Anatomist*—its movement from comic calm to melodramatic emotion (with a strong flavour of tragedy) and back again to the balance of comedy—reminds us of some of the tragi-comic technique of some Shakespeare plays like *Much Ado about Nothing* and *The Merchant of Venice.* The use of the chorus in *A Sleeping Clergyman* to comment, anticipate the action, and provide some kind of moral viewpoint is a more obvious link with the Greek theatre;

but an even more striking theatrical feature used to highlight the major theme here is the exploitation of Dr. Marshall as choric figure, manipulator, and character in his own right. In some ways he may be compared with Prospero in *The Tempest* and the Duke in *Measure for Measure*; but in that he is the choric means whereby the past, present and future rôles and history of the Camerons are dramatically fused, he fulfils the same function as the Chorus in Aeschylus' *Oresteia*. Inspector MacIvor appearing at the end of *Dr. Angelus* is less a choric character than a manipulator—a *deus ex machina* come to bring about some kind of resolution. He has also something of the quality of a messenger—like Death in the Morality Play of Everyman. *The Anatomist,* exploiting Knox as a figure of evil amid the vice and macabre atmosphere of the Three Tuns and mortuary settings, achieves a kind of mediaeval quality. *A Sleeping Clergyman* also, exploiting squalor and vice in the early parts, and positive values towards the end, presents the evil and the good in the manner of the Morality. But it is in *Dr. Angelus* that we find the most clearly stated opposition between good and evil in the figures of Johnson and Angelus, and the strongest impressions of an Everyman struggling towards the good.

It is noteworthy that all these three doctor plays are founded on real-life events that took place in the nineteenth century. All are examples of how Bridie could transmute the raw material of medical and legal history to produce structured dramatic pieces. All are examples of how he could combine naturalistic method with melodrama and non-realism to make his moral statements. The odd thing is that the real-life situations from which he took the outlines and some of the details are in themselves thoroughly melodramatic.

On the face of it Bridie does not appear to have much in

common with Shakespeare in the handling and heightening of language. In dialogue, he uses prose that has a hard contemporary ring; and although there are flourishes of rhetoric from Knox, Cameron and Angelus in their high moments, there is no overt 'poetic' style. It is rather at moments of insight where a character reveals himself— sometimes in monologue, sometimes in soliloquy—that we can trace something of a similarity with Shakespearean technique. In *The Anatomist* Knox at an inner climactic moment in his conversation with Amelia in Act Three reveals his feeling of guilt; and in *A Sleeping Clergyman* similar moments emerge in Marshall's meditations and prophetic passages. In *Dr. Angelus* we have striking examples of these revealing monologues—Angelus's discourse on Bacon's Idols, Johnson's dream-fantasy, Angelus' monologue over the unconscious figure of Johnson.

The doctor plays reveal a remarkable flexibility in technique within the mould of apparently realist drama. They provide a clear illustration of Bridie's dramatic methods and his insights into the aspirations, attractions, and dangers of the medical profession. Their structure is found to be governed not only by conventional or classical and mediaeval influences but also by a moral intensity that arises out of a creative re-shaping of the raw material of medical and legal history. There are Scottish qualities in atmosphere and language, as may be seen; but the strongest Scottish characteristics of these plays reside precisely in this moral intensity that reflects the struggle between the evil and the good.

CHAPTER TWO

Two Biblical Plays

IT IS NATURAL that Bridie should have developed a great
interest in the Old Testament and Apocrypha stories set in
the ancient Jewish and Assyrian territories of the near
East. For one thing his Scottish upbringing would have
given him a solid grounding in the Bible; for another his
experiences in Mesopotamia, Persia and Constantinople
must have provided him with a knowledge of the settings
he was to use in his plays. His first biblical play *Tobias
and the Angel,* written and first produced in 1930, was
only a moderate success when it was performed in London
in 1932; but since then it has become perhaps the most
popular of the Bridie plays. The second biblical play
Jonah and the Whale (1932) suffered from having too
many characters and supers, and was re-written as a radio
play *The Sign of the Prophet Jonah.* The third version
Jonah 3, with nineteen characters instead of twenty-six as
in the original, produced ten years later at the theatre of
the Unnamed Society in Manchester, was well received,
but is regarded as inferior to *Tobias,* being rather wordy
and lacking dramatic qualities. In 1937 Bridie again
turned to the Apocrypha and wrote a play based on the
book *The History of Susanna* which he called *Susannah
and the Elders.* This play was given only three
performances in London when it was first written, and
since then it has been performed only occasionally. It
appears to have been popular at Pitlochry, and certainly
deserves to be better known.

The two biblical plays I deal with are *Tobias and the
Angel* and *Susannah and the Elders,* both dominated by
men or women of God, who may be prophet, angel, or

ordinary mortal—Daniel, Raphael, Tobit, Susannah. These are contrasting pieces, the one humorous, the other tragical, the one having as its centrepiece a presiding archangel comically human at times, the other having as its chief character an upright woman shamefully wronged.

Bridie himself in his author's note describes *Tobias and the Angel* (1930) as "a plain-sailing dramatic transcription of the charming old tale told in the Book of Tobit in the Apocrypha"; and indeed this play does keep close to the original story of "the troubles of Tobit", "the adventures of Tobias", and "Tobias's homecoming", strangely enough the titles of the divisions of the story as given in *The New English Bible with the Apocrypha,* 1970, which Bridie, working forty years earlier on the Authorised Version, structurally anticipates in his play. The three acts which correspond to these divisions could well bear these titles.

Bridie moulds the material into lively dramatic form and uses modern idiom, although his author's note describes the language used as "a speech belonging to no particular period". Like the writers of the mediaeval Mystery plays, Bridie makes a human document out of a story from scripture. Indeed, from the time of the first performance of *Tobias* at the Cambridge Festival Theatre in November 1930, critics have tended to speak of its "lovable" qualities and characters. It may well be, as Bridie himself suggests, that the qualities and 'opinions' of his characters owe something to their originals; but it is obvious that more changes and developments have been made than are mentioned in the author's note. Tobit is a much more human, more modest person in the play; Tobias emerges as a young man much less sure of himself than in the Apocrypha story; and Raphael is less of a shadowy divinity and more of a human figure with his vanity, sense of humour, and air of authority. Bridie

42

admits he has altered "the opinions of Sara"; and certainly Sara in the play has a greater range of emotion and variety of mood. It is difficult to see anything in the original to suggest the hint of Cleopatra that is discernible in her at the beginning of Act II.

An important change has been made too in thematic emphasis. In the Book of Tobit it is clear that the prayers of Tobit and of Sara are to be answered. Tobit is to be released from the misery of his blindness and Sara from her bondage to the devil Asmodeus. These things do happen in Bridie's play, but they do not emerge as the main events or themes. Helen L. Luyben, considering the moral of *Tobias and the Angel,* is doubtful if the purpose is to reward Tobit's or Tobias's virtue. A.C. Ward makes the point, in his introduction to the 1931 edition of the play, that it was not written "as a morality play intended to teach us how to behave"; but he goes on to speak of Bridie's interest in "mankind's need of the Good Life". Although it is true that at the end of the play Tobit has the satisfaction of having his son restored and of becoming prosperous again, we know from the first act that he has given up material ambitions and that he is really only interested in the Good Life. The restoration of his sight has its symbolic significance: Tobit lives to *see* his aim fulfilled—Tobias's maturing into a man with a developing sense of family and religious duty. The structural emphasis of the play is on Tobias rather than Tobit: the first act contrasts Tobit's balance and sanity with Tobias's lack of confidence and immaturity; the third act demonstrates the change that has been wrought in Tobias: he has even become the means whereby his father's sight is restored. Thematically then the play is less concerned with the reward for Tobit's virtue than with demonstrating the need for the education that comes of guided experience. Tobias's journey is a kind of pilgrimage undertaken by an Everyman with an archangel for guide.

The Book of Tobit, with its three clearly defined parts—Tobit's life in Nineveh as a blind man, Tobias's adventures with Raphael and Sara, the home-coming marked by the curing of Tobit's blindness—is ideal material for transformation into a Bridie three-act play. We have dealt briefly with the first and third acts: it is interesting now to turn to the second act and consider its structural effect. Here we have a startling contrast to the opening mood. The instability and the dangerous attraction of women are presented in a setting of superstition and violence—a dramatic contrast to the stability and security of the Tobit personality and setting. The secular yet impersonal tone established by the singing and dancing at Hamadan contrasts too with the religious yet human tone of the Nineveh setting. Sara in her Cleopatra mood dominates the first part at least of this middle movement as Tobit dominates the opening movement; and it may be said that Raphael comes more and more to dominate the last movement to leave the impression of the god-like and the supernatural that we find at the end of the story of Tobias's homecoming in the Apocrypha.

Tobit, Sara, Raphael then are bound up with the structure of the play: each has an influence on Tobias in the course of his pilgrimage. Helen L. Luyben thinks that Sara and Raphael may be working to make a man out of Tobias, yet, as she points out, "Sara's motivation is in Asmoday, Raphael's opponent, who is one of Jahveh's fallen angels". Before we deal with the key conflict between Raphael and Asmoday we should note how Raphael's influence on Tobias differs from Sara's. Raphael is the objective guide and inspirer of Tobias whereas Sara provides his subjective inspiration. Raphael's comments and commands have a schoolmasterly formality:

44

> Pull yourself together . . . You are to marry the
> girl . . . Now be a good boy and try to be a credit to
> me . . .

Sara's lines have romantic and emotional power:

> I love you too, Tobias. That is why this time is
> worse than ever before . . . Go away, my darling . . .
> Asmoday will never allow me happiness.

The conflict between Raphael and Asmoday is at the
heart of the middle movement of the play. Asmoday
represents the irrational, the occult, the grotesque element
operating against mankind. He represents destructive
powers as Raphael represents creative rational powers.
Asmoday's spirit hovers over the first part of Act II. The
opening song sung by Sherah is full of references to violent
creatures—the jackal, the dog, the jaguar; but by the end
of the second scene of Act II Sherah is singing of positive
things—the season of leaves and sheaves, and the
dulcimers that celebrate the end of Asmoday. In between
has come the struggle between Raphael and Asmoday,
presented as a Pantomime (Bridie's own word) partly in
dumb show, partly in dialogue, and ending in Raphael's
complete victory. Here in the heart of the play the
symbolic triumph of the Good Angel over the Bad is
staged; and it is to be noted that Bridie's dramatic method
is essentially comic here. By Raphael's treatment and
judgment Asmoday becomes an object of ridicule:

> He never washes . . . they had a nickname for him in
> the College of Cherubim . . . they nicknamed him the
> Stinker.

This conflict between Raphael and Asmoday is counterpointed by the maturing of Sara and Tobias through their love. Working under Raphael's influence, Tobias becomes the instrument of Sara's liberation from the Asmoday legend and superstition; and Sara herself by her belief in Tobias helps him in his transformation from boy to man. Raphael's magisterial scolding of Sara for daring to fall in love with an archangel "six thousand years" her senior has been appreciated for its wit; but we have to remember also how this whole sequence fits into the structure of the play. It occurs in the transition scene III.1 before the return to Nineveh. It *is* part of the comic texture of the play but it has to be viewed also in the context of the re-education of Sara and the preparation for her position as Tobias's wife. We are here at the midway stage of a journey back to humanity: it is natural that she should be looking back over her shoulder at angels after she has been rescued from Asmoday. She has yet to be broken from her habit of seeing visions and being attracted to demons and gods.

Raphael's rôle is central to the play. He links the naturalistic with the supernatural elements and is gradually seen as the force that illustrates the main theme. The play moves from its base of humility, sanity and love, where he plays a peripheral part, to an unsteady centre highly coloured, volatile, vicious, where he becomes active as manipulator, inspirer and destroyer. Spells have to be broken; and the conflict between Asmoday and Raphael himself has to be presented in terms of mediaeval Morality and resolved in terms of Aristophanic pantomime. The first act presents the problem of the mundane Tobias and the need for his education; the second act introduces as counterpoint the problem of the romantic Sara and the need for her rescue and education. Raphael is the stage manager manipulating events so that he may finally confront his enemy, guiding and training his pupils and

46

leading them back to sanity and harmony. The third act completes the transformation of Sara and Tobias, restores us to the godly sanity of Tobit, and, taking the emphasis off the temporal problems of the characters, extends the range and dramatic power of the play by throwing the figure of Raphael into high theatrical relief. Despite his magisterial tone Raphael has been concerned more with encouraging his protégés to take action and develop and realise their potentialities than with preaching at them. Tobias finds powers within himself that he has not been aware of; Sara discovers in herself a humanity and a wisdom that liberate her from her pose as *femme fatale* and from her immature beliefs. Raphael turns out to be a kind of schoolmaster after all, but the better kind of schoolmaster who brings out latent qualities and inspires his pupils to take action and work out a way of living. His divine quality as revealed at the end of the play is a reminder of the mysterious source of mental and physical energy in the most ordinary of human creatures.

Tobias and the Angel turns out to be a subtler play than we had at first imagined. It has more than "lovable" characters, a human archangel, and a charming story wittily presented. In illustrating the creative powers of good and ridiculing the powers of evil, it reminds us that it is only when we are liberated from personal preoccupations and limitations that we can glimpse forces and possibilities beyond ourselves:

We have been visited.

Yet the play remains a human document. The character of Tobit is the more striking for being set off by the character of his wife Anna. The dialogue in Act I in which Anna attacks her husband's over-virtuous ways has the lively quality and characterisation we find in the Mystery play in the Chester Pageant that features Noah and his wife. The exchanges between father and son in the first act illustrate the mental gap between the mature and the callow; and the love passages between Sara and Tobias at the end of Act II and in the first scene of Act III have an ease and a simplicity as well as emotional outbursts. The relationship between Tobias and Sara contains one of the keys to understanding the message of the play. In their love and need for each other lies their liberation from immaturity and fear. Under Raphael's guidance they can resist the dangers of Asmoday and attain a harmony in their lives. The master touch is in the human portrait within the manipulating figure of Raphael. The wit and irony, the imperiousness and inspiration, we would expect from an archangel; but there is also that touch of pride, that supreme self-confidence which he reveals before and after the Pantomime in Act II, as he first anticipates and then celebrates his victory over Asmoday.

The language is simple, direct and dramatic. It can range from the easy colloquial style found throughout the play in passages between father and son, between Sara and Tobias, even between Raphael and Tobias, to the pseudo-melodramatic style used by the Bandit in I II (and later imitated by Tobias himself). Raphael's language has a formal quality that matches his wit and irony; but when he is off guard or feeling pleased with himself he too can be colloquial and direct. At the end of the play when he reassumes the rôle of archangel he uses a dignified yet simple biblical style that recalls the language used by Tobit in the evening hymn that concludes the first scene of Act I. What we may call the 'poetry' of the play is more difficult to deal with. It is an elusive element that bubbles up in various places—quietly at the end of the first scene of Act I after Tobit's hymn, formally in Sherah's songs, ritualistically in the passage in Act II where Raguel gives

48

Sara to Tobias in marriage—where the words are lifted direct from the Authorised Version of the Apocrypha. This 'poetic' quality emerges rather self-consciously and artificially in Tobias's praise of Sara at the end of the first scene of Act III—"Your eyes are like two brown pigeons sheltering behind purple hibiscus petals . . .", but more genuinely and strikingly in Sara's final speech at the end of the play describing Raphael's appearances:

> I saw him pale, like a ghost . . . Today I saw him like a drifting mist.

In assessing the achievement of *Tobias and the Angel*, then, we have to consider how Bridie has varied his linguistic patterns, moulded his material from the Apocrypha, and harmonised the different styles and planes to make a unified whole. The view held by some critics that Bridie was not interested in form and had difficulty with his last acts is disproved by a scrutiny of this play alone. Even a cursory examination of its dramatic construction shows how *Tobias* moves steadily to a thematically and theatrically apt finale.

In its three-part structure *Tobias and the Angel* is similar to *The Anatomist*. The first and third parts are set in the home territory of Nineveh and dominated by the benign moral order of Tobit; the second is set in the "testing" territory of Hamadan, pervaded by restlessness and questing, and highly coloured, as we have noted, by the personality of Sara. Although at first sight *Tobias* looks like another play constructed in simple ternary from *aba,* there is an important modification that shows Bridie moving from the strict three-part formula to a more flexible form. The second scene of the first act begins the movement of the play away from its first to its second centre: it is set "on the banks of the Tigris, a day's march from Nineveh"; and the second scene of the second act similarly begins the movement back from the second to the first centre: it is set in "a Khan near Kifri". In this movement out of and back to a first base or home territory, with transition scenes, *Tobias* recalls the structure of such Shakespeare comedies as *A Midsummer Night's Dream* and *The Winter's Tale.*

In the best traditions of comedy, Bridie is concerned in the finale of *Tobias and the Angel* with staging restoration and recognition scenes. The son is restored to his parents; sight is restored to the old man; and Sara is recognised as the daughter-in-law brought home by Tobias. Finally the focus moves round to Raphael not yet come on stage. Tobias in a throw-away, conversational cliché foreshadows the recognition of the rôle "Azarias" (the name assumed by Raphael) has been playing:

> Azarias has been a sort of guardian angel to me, daddy. First he made me kill a devil-fish . . . Oh, and hundreds of things . . . and he . . . taught me how to cure your blindness.

Then comes the Bridie-esque comic anticlimax exploiting a detail of the original Apocryphal legend:

> *Tobit.* And all for one drachma a day. What an invaluable man.

Raphael makes his final appearance climbing the bank of rubble and taking up a formal position above Tobit and Tobias. Tobit raises the matter of the great debt they owe him but the answer "You owe me nothing" is iterated with a developing power. Raphael's speech comes as a prayer or incantation:

It is good to praise Jahveh and to exalt His name. Jahveh has heard your prayers and has seen your deeds that were themselves prayers.

At the end the non-realist technique strengthens the message and effectively interprets the legend: ·

> *He throws off his cloak*
> I am Raphael, one of the seven angels, who present
>   the prayers of the Saints before the throne . . .
> You have seen a vision.
> Now, therefore, give God thanks . . .

This is the final *anagnorisis* that explains everything, the final touch of the supernatural that is accompanied— *by a blinding flash and a chord of stage music.* After Raphael's disappearance, there are excited comments by the other characters which were criticised by some reviewers but which are in my opinion strikingly within the tone of wonder created by Raphael's prayer, a tone given ultimate expression by Sara:

> I saw him pale, like a ghost, and when he walked in front of you I saw you through his body. Today I saw him like a drifting mist.

The emphasis is appropriately off the personal and firmly on the strange forces behind life and eternity. The ending thus demonstrates the great inner theme that has been gradually built up and developed throughout the action—the transformation that education and experience of a spiritual nature can bring about.

Bridie devotes about four pages of his Preface in the volume *Susannah and the Elders and Other Plays* to an explanation and interpretation of *Susannah and the Elders* (1937). The story comes from the Apocrypha in the Authorised Version in the book called *The History of Susanna,* but Bridie made two important changes. His Elders are not Jews but Assyrians; and this change, as he explains, enabled him to build into his play "an eternally topical decoration"—the nationalistic feelings of the Jews in general and the Daniel group in particular towards their Babylonian captors. The second important change is an addition—the introduction of the young Greek traveller Dionysos, the "hedonistic young man about town" who falls in love with Susannah, a character that may be said to have grown out of the purely imaginary young man mentioned by the Elders in their testimony against Susanna. With tongue in cheek Bridie added that Dionysos "in his capacity of *raisonneur*" provided a link between the play and the intelligentsia (the London dramatic critics). Certainly the discussions initiated or developed by Dionysos have a certain intellectual appeal—on religion, on love; but more important for the structure of the play is his function as rival to the Elders and young would-be lover to Susannah. Dionysos serves to throw into relief Susannah's virtue and strength of character at certain points in the play; but also he tends to steal some at least of the sympathy the author was hoping to build up for the Elders. The impression of his attractive personality is established in the first scene where he debates wittily with his judges, and it continues to develop through the middle movement of the play where he attempts to make love to Susannah, right up to the final garden scene where he argues pleasantly with the majordomo and is dismissed by Susannah. His death off-stage has the quality of a sacrifice, and, being synchronised with the unmasking of the Elders, has the effect of increasing the sympathy the audience already feels for him.

52

Bridie was emphatic that he wanted sympathy for the Elders; and oddly enough he thought the invention of Dionysos would help. He wrote in his Preface: "If there had been no Greek, my audience would have lost all sympathy with the Elders and at once accepted them as villains". This matter of arousing sympathy is closely bound up with the more important question as to what are the main themes of the play. Bridie himself gave various clues. He said his play "may be looked upon as a moral story, rebuking wickedness and glorifying virtue". He drew attention to the central importance of Susannah: the play tells "a plain story of a persecuted heroine and of the confounding of her persecutors". He also hinted at the importance of the politico-religious theme that runs through the play: it may be read "as tribute . . . to the Jews, to the genius of Daniel, to the jurisprudence of the Captivity, to the mercy of God". His reference to the story in the Koran of Harut and Marut, the two angels who as old men became corrupt on earth and ran after Zohara-Aphrodite, is clearly relevant to his own interpretation of the original story. He places emphasis on the Elders deliberately, for he believes that it is in the Elders' dilemma that the tragedy resides. He elaborates on the kind of "silly and outrageous acts" that distinguished old men are sometimes driven into through the wandering of desire, acts that have sometimes tragic implications. He says too that he deliberately built up the impression of Kashdak and Kabbittu as "modern, cultivated, respected and respectable old civil servants of the class easily recognised as gentlemen", so that their fall and presumably also our sympathy with them should be the greater.

It is interesting to compare an author's original aims and intentions with the actual way the play operates on the stage and affects an audience. It is true that we at first see the Judges at work as respectable Assyrian Elders; it is true that they respond to Susannah's request that Dionysos' life should be spared; and it is true that Joachim and Susannah believe them to be respectable, friendly and charming old men. But in the unfolding of the drama it is their less attractive qualities that are thrown up. Kashdak, in agreeing to spare Dionysos' life, does so in cynical mood, revealing himself a man of little belief. Both he and Kabbittu protest too much, overstressing their old age as the guarantee of their respectability. Indeed, the play at certain key points brings out the hypocrisy of the Elders— at the end of the fourth scene in Act II when Kashdak persuades Susannah to use the pool, in their accidental meeting in II V in which they discuss Susannah's visit to the garden, and particularly in II VI just before they confront Susannah in the garden. Although Bridie in his Preface says or implies that he does not want the Elders to be "accepted as villains", the dramatic build-up is to the point towards the end of the second act (II VI) where Kashdak is revealed as an arch-villain, the more villainous for being cloaked with power and respectability.

Kurt Wittig speaks of the tragic atmosphere created by "presenting the story . . . as seen by the Elders"; but the movement of the play is away from the viewpoint of the Elders towards sympathy with Susannah in her isolation. If Dionysos were a central character, then his death would convert the play to tragedy; but the action concentrates more and more on Susannah as central character, and the moment of her greatest agony, towards which the whole play is structured, has a tragic potential which is not realised and tragic possibilities which are dramatically averted.

Susannah and the Elders is more akin to Shakespeare's tragi-comic romances like *Measure for Measure* and *The Winter's Tale* than to his tragedies. Indeed, in theme and in the treatment of heroine and would-be villain Bridie's play has strong affinities with *Measure for Measure* in particular. Both plays contrast legalism with mercy and humanity, corruption in high office with unblemished virtue. It is true that Isabella in *Measure* is not always the apostle of humanity or mercy as Susannah more consistently is, although by the end she has become so in asking mercy for Angelo; but it is also true that both heroines maintain a chaste attitude to love. Above all there is striking similarity between Isabella helpless in being frustrated by the power and prestige of Angelo and Susannah helpless in being betrayed by the respectable Elders. When the heroine threatens to expose the villain, the response of the villain is identical in both plays:

> *Angelo*: Who will believe thee, Isabel? (*Measure*)
> *Kashdak*: Who will believe you? (*Susannah*)

There are strong resemblances between Kashdak's cold respectable manner and Angelo's best judicial pose; and when they are unmasked and at their most libidinous the Elders show the same cynicism and unscrupulous misuse of power as Angelo does. Up to near the end Susannah remains the chief character: she, not the Elders, undergoes suffering and trial; sympathy is built up for her, not the Elders.

Important though the Susannah theme is, however, we must try to see it in its relationship to the Daniel theme. Both the Authorised Version and the *New English Bible* emphasise the importance of Daniel's actions in the story; and it is significant that the *N.E.B.* by its heading *Daniel and Susanna* appears to stress the relationship between the two that Bridie dramatises so sharply. Bridie himself, it will be remembered, hinted at the importance of this politico-religious theme, when he referred to "the genius of Daniel" and "the jurisprudence of the Captivity".

Through the words and actions of Daniel and his group we are constantly reminded of the conflict between the Jews and their Assyrian conquerors. This theme is treated peripherally to begin with: Daniel and his friends make their first appearances on the edges of the play—in a tailpiece to the first scene where they confront and insult the Elders, and in the street scene I II where Daniel's resentment against the Assyrians is revealed in all its fanaticism:

I shall care for and nourish the rage of the Jew till the last Chaldean brat has his head dashed to bits on these cobblestones . . .

The politico-religious theme moves nearer the centre of the play in the final scene of the first act where Daniel argues with Susannah and warns her of the dangers of fraternising with the Elders. Here the two main themes seem to merge: Daniel is the interpreter of the Law of the Jews, the Prophet and the political leader of the Jews in captivity, whereas Susannah represents the spirit of reconciliation and forgiveness. Daniel's importance in the structure of the drama begins to become clear at this point. By his religious insight and political vehemence against the Assyrians he is able to anticipate the evil events at the end of Act II. He describes the Elders as "full of experience and mystery and wickedness"; and in his final exchange with Susannah he makes the prophetic comment that bears directly on the high climax of the attempted seduction:

Even in old Judges the lusts of the flesh take a long time to die.

In the trial scene in Act III, Daniel moves to the centre

56

of the play; and on the face of it, it seems right that the Prophet of God should use his skill to expose evil and right a wrong. It seems appropriate too that at this high climax we should have a demonstration of the "justice" or "mercy of God" theme. But there is an impersonal quality about Daniel's action here. He is interested in the purely legalistic aspect of the case: he harshly refuses to accept Susannah's thanks because he has been acting against the Assyrians rather than for Susannah. The two main themes do not merge here: they are flashed together for contrast. On the one hand we have Daniel as the skilled lawyer fulfilling his function as Prophet of the Jews; on the other Susannah representing humanity and belief in the mercy of God.

The portrayal of the fanatical Daniel and the puritanical Susannah suggests that this play is not without its relevance to Bridie's Scottish background and culture. Daniel, as well as being prophet and lawyer, is also the militant leader of a small nation overshadowed by a larger one: his nationalistic self-consciousness as a Jew has something of the self-consciousness of the modern Scot whose culture and way of life are in danger of being obliterated by anglicisation. The fanatical attitude to his firmly held religious ideas may also be taken as a reflection of the attitude of the Scot to his Presbyterianism. Susannah too in her particular brand of puritanism reflects something of the Scottish attitude to morality; but she and her husband Joachim, in their desire to be friendly and socialise with their Assyrian hosts, may also represent the Anglo-Scots who are prepared to compromise rather than stand out for full national identity. Bridie does seem here, in the words of Kurt Wittig, to project "the problem of modern Anglo-Scottish tensions back into a Biblical past", and in doing so, to endow it "with universal significance".

In view of the importance of Susannah and the Elders in its range of ideas, in its dramatic power, and in its relevance to Anglo-Scottish and universal political problems, it is strange that critics seem to have ignored it or to have been little moved by it. Helen L. Luyben, apart from listing it in her chronology and bibliography, makes no mention of it at all. Winifred Bannister, after quoting Bridie's prefatory remarks about the "several different kinds of story in the play", concludes "he has failed to involve us deeply with the theme", and finds the play "remains contrived". She also thinks Bridie may have made a mistake in choosing as heroine a woman so chaste. On the other hand, Ursula Gerber in her more detailed study of the play stresses its compact and poetical nature, as well as its structural and thematic power. She goes on to comment on aspects of Susannah's character that link her, not so much with Isabella and Hermione as I would do, as with Portia and Beatrice—in her playfulness and sense of fun. Miss Gerber shows a keen appreciation of Bridie's irony; and I notice that she too postulates a discrepancy between the actual effect of the play and Bridie's intention: ". . . eine eindeutige Diskrepanz zwischen dem tatsächlichen Effekt des Stückes und Bridies Intention."

In my view *Susannah and the Elders* is a play worthy of being surveyed afresh and subjected to the kind of dramatic visualisation that should enable us to work out its method and message. If we fail to take it seriously as a major Bridie play, we shall miss important aspects of Bridie's craft as dramatist and important examples of the way he handles themes that have a universal as well as a Scottish application. My own survey suggests that it is skilfully constructed rather than contrived, and that Susannah herself emerges as a rational, humane, lively and attractive personality rather than a dull Lady Chastity. Perhaps, like Dorothea Brooke in *Middlemarch* and

Isabel Archer in *Portrait of a Lady,* she is betrayed by being too trustful and too intellectual; but at no point do I find her chastity dulling the edge of characterisation or reducing the pace of the drama.

At a first glance, *Susannah and the Elders* seems to be structured as a three-act play; but on closer examination one finds that these acts are more like movements, each with a unity within its diversity. Bridie here seems to be using the more flexible form of an episodic play. His first act falls into three scenes, the middle one to be presented in front of a traverse curtain; his second act is divided into six scenes, two of these also to be played before the traverse according to the stage direction. The third act is complete in itself within the setting of the Judges' garden. Although Bridie has specifically referred to the use of a drop or traverse curtain for ease in staging, it is clear that the play is suited to the kind of flexible semi-permanent or unlocalised setting that is used in modern productions of Shakespeare. The three-part structure of *Susannah* also seems to reflect aspects of the neo-Terentian pattern with its division into *protasis, epitasis* and *catastrophe.* The first act or movement is shaped like the *protasis* with its build-up to a preliminary climax—the sparing of Dionysos' life, and the foreshadowing of the main climax by Daniel. The second leads up to the highest climactic points of the "high *epitasis*"—Dionysos' death and Susannah's betrayal by the Elders. The third has the unravelling structure of the traditional *catastrophe* in its court-of-justice scene which leads to the final resolution—the proving of Susannah's innocence.

As a final attempt to understand Bridie's method and message in this play, it might be worth while trying to visualise how this finale works on the stage. The final court-of-law scene, presided over by the old man Latazakar and presented with the full panoply of the

Babylonian College of Justice, is a striking contrast to the first court-of-justice scene in which Susannah was an honoured guest. The Elders' treachery is presented in terms of false witness vouched by Kabbittu; and there is grim irony in the method of execution prescribed for Susannah—immersion in the reservoir. In Susannah's statement of her innocence and in her appeal to the justice of God there is something of the strength and firmness of purpose shown by Hermione in her trial scene in *The Winter's Tale*:

> I have done none of these things of which they accuse me . . . O Everlasting God! . . . You know what these things mean and how they come about. You know that they have lied and why they have lied, and that I must die for their lies. In your mind alone there is justice and goodness and right. O Everlasting Lord, receive my spirit!

It is at this point, when Susannah has sunk to the ground and the tipstaves are about to seize her, that Daniel makes his dramatic intervention in words lifted direct from the Authorised Version:

> I am clear of the blood of this woman!

In his taking over the case Daniel shows something of the self-assurance of Portia in the trial scene of *The Merchant of Venice;* and in his challenge to Latazakar he shows something of Shylock's defiant appeal to the laws of Venice:

> Latazakar, take your state and re-open the Court. If you will not listen to me, you will make yourself a derision and a hissing to the King and his people and to

the multitude of their children for ever and ever.

Daniel does indeed show himself a wise young judge: in accusing the Elders he appeals to the King's law and claims his privilege as a member of the Court. Having brought out the weaknesses in Kabbittu's evidence and demonstrated the Elders' suspicious presence in the garden, he then proceeds to draw out of Kabbittu his version of the fictitious Susannah-Dionysos assignation:

> *Daniel.* They were under a tree, I think you said?
> *Kabbittu.* Yes.
> *Daniel.* Which tree?
> *Kabbittu.* A mastik tree.
> *Daniel.* To the south of the pond?
> *Kabbittu.* Yes.

Kashdak is recalled and led by Daniel to make completely contradictory statements about the alleged assignation. At the end of the cross-examination Daniel emerges triumphant, and his scorn for the Assyrians comes out clearly in his condemnation of the Elders:

> Go down to Hell, liar and murderer! Go with your foul associate. And you, Lord Latazakar, Judge of Babylon, on your head and on your allegiance to your king, hasten their steps.

Two further rises in the flow of the play illustrate Bridie's skill in maintaining thematic interest to the end. The first comes at the beginning of the coda when Susannah attempts to thank Daniel for saving her life. Here Daniel's impersonal prophetic quality contrasts strikingly with Susannah's warm-hearted and devout nature:

Susannah. Daniel, ... I shall never forget your goodness . . . Dear Daniel!

Daniel. Has it not been revealed to you yet that you are compact of folly and danger? . . . Go home and pray. You will not kill me as you killed the Greek. I am no old man to run to my death because of you . . . Go home and pray.

Susannah. I don't understand you. I think you must be mad. I shall pray for you.

The second comes near the end when Daniel's group are interrupted in their mocking commentary on the fate of the Elders by Daniel himself more concerned with tracing in nature divine pattern and intention:

No doubt but it was good . . . There is the rain at last. The dry earth will drink and awaken and the air will be full of great odours. The Lord has spoken to all life that it may rise again.

When Meshach wants to make the reference to God's speaking through Daniel more specific, Daniel reveals the doubt in his mind that brings an ambiguity to the concluding dialogue:

Meshach. As He spoke already today, Daniel, through your mind.

Daniel. I hope he did, Meshach. I do not know.

These last words of Daniel and his long look back at the inner garden (as indicated by the final stage direction) suggest he is having doubts about his own skill as Judge and Prophet of God, and recall the words of the Reader in the Prologue of the play:

Search yourselves that you may do (judge) justly.

The first striking feature of these biblical plays is their achievement in presenting and making dramatically interesting portraits of morally good people. In *Tobias and the Angel* Bridie not only succeeds in making Tobit an attractive humorous and religious character: he builds the personality firmly into the design of the play. At the end of the first scene Tobit takes over from Anna the task of preparing Tobias for his journey; at the end of the play he presides over his restored and enlarged family and accepts naturally the revelation that they have been visited. In *Susannah and the Elders* Susannah's personality is presented in such a dynamic way that her generosity and kindness bring about in the first scene the important action of the freeing of Dionysos. Susannah has a more dangerous sense of humour than Tobit, although Tobit's tendency to overdo his acts of kindness frequently lands him in trouble. Susannah's playfulness and sense of fun, allied to her trusting nature, lead her to develop her friendship with the Elders to the point where she becomes an easy victim in the garden. Yet it is her very strength of character that makes her moment of agony so dramatically effective. Her refusal to yield brings out the truth of the situation and the hidden evil in the Elders.

There is in these plays a quality of "romance" that intensifies in the middle movement. In *Tobias* we move from the humdrum realist environment of Tobit's hovel in Nineveh with its domestic concerns to the highly exciting environment of Hamadan with its lurking violence, its singing and dancing, its legend about Asmoday's power over Sara. In *Susannah* the move is to the Judges' garden with its isolating walls, its vaguely menacing beauty, its air of remoteness, its pool. It is here too that the violence breaks out in the quarrel between the Elders and in the killing of Dionysos; and it is here that the highly dramatic action of the attempted violation of Susannah takes place.

Both plays are concerned with firmly held religious beliefs that are linked with nationalistic feelings. Tobit's devotion to his national religion makes him defy the harsh alien laws that forbid Jews to go out and bury their dead. (His position has something in common with Antigone's.) Both Tobit and Susannah are revealed at certain points as unshakable in their religious beliefs—Tobit at the end of the first scene of *Tobias,* Susannah at the moment of agony in her trial scene. Two contrasting attitudes to religion and humanity come from Raphael and Daniel: Raphael's is the magisterial attitude, dispassionate, God-like, yet showing an interest in human beings. Daniel's is the attitude of the zealot, single-minded, dictatorial, scarcely concerned with the human situation. Both have their relevance to the Scottish character. Raphael is the Scottish schoolmaster, pompous, kindly, conceited, witty; Daniel is the bigoted Calvinist and the committed nationalist, single-minded, implacable, dour and moody.

Tobias and the Angel and *Susannah and the Elders* illustrate Bridie's tendency to break away from the strict three-act form; and they demonstrate how he could mould the material of the Apocrypha into dramatic form. In *Susannah* he uses an episodic form within which he presents his drama in ten scenes that are not tied throughout to any one physical setting but are rather built up according to dramatic patterns. Yet he can exploit the sense of place, the exotic background of his Apocrypha material. Thus in *Tobias* he sees the dramatic possibilities of a move from mundane Nineveh to romantic Hamadan; and in *Susannah* he exploits for dramatic purposes both the court-of-law scenes and the central garden scene.

One of the most interesting features of these plays is

64

Bridie's developing use of the devices of poetry to heighten the drama, enrich the background, or intensify thematic power. Songs and music are introduced at certain points—in *Tobias* to stress lurking violence or the triumph of the Good Angel, in *Susannah* to hint at the attractions and dangers of love. In *Susannah* the garden, the moon, and the refreshing rain become important as symbols, and in *Tobias* animal imagery is set against the gentler aspects of nature to emphasise the drama of situation and character.

Bridie's biblical plays combine realist dialogue and situation with religious and romantic outbursts and visions; and the combination succeeds in giving us impressions of humanity struggling with its animal instincts and its pretensions to intelligence and divinity.

CHAPTER THREE

TWO DRAMATIC PORTRAITS

BRIDIE SEEMED TO enjoy writing plays round a personality, a bright or arresting character, a typically Scottish figure. There are at least three minor plays that illustrate his skill in bringing alive dynamic or strange people on the stage. The first— *The Forrigan Reel* (1944)—is a rollicking study of Donald MacAlpin, a daft laddie who has the gift of healing through his powers of dancing. In the version described as "A Ballad Opera" it failed to impress London critics, but in its original form as a play it was a great success with Scottish and Irish audiences. The second—*John Knox* (1947)—was originally written for the Edinburgh Festival. Knox must have seemed an ideal subject for the kind of character-drama Bridie liked to attempt; but in this instance the history and the character seem to have proved too bulky and overpowering for the dramatic form and technique. The third—*Gog and Magog* (1948)—is based on the story of McGonagall, the Dundee doggerel poet. It is a study of a pathetic figure who considers himself poet and tragedian; and it has an element of caricature which contrasts with its human pathos.

Bridie succeeds more consistently with his portraits of professional men. We have seen how well he can sketch a medical man in his milieu and yet bring out individual characteristics: *The Switchback, The Anatomist, A Sleeping Clergyman, Dr. Angelus* all contain convincing portraits of doctors. But in these plays the practice of medicine is as important thematically as the personality. They are medical dramas as much as portraits. Bridie was however interested in presenting portraits of other professional men—ministers and teachers as well as doctors. The portrait plays that have proved most popular and durable in my view are *Mr. Bolfry*, a study of a minister with a devil inside him, and *Mr Gillie*, a study of an idealist schoolmaster. These seem to me companion pieces worthy of detailed attention. Both present Scottish characters who exemplify typically Scottish preoccupations with religion and education.

Some critics believe that *Mr Bolfry* (1943) is essentially a study of the devil and evil. Winifred Bannister said that Bridie in *Mr Bolfry* had achieved "the most delectable Devil in his volume"; and Gerald Weales described the play as "a serious diabolic comedy". Ursula Gerber was interested in the similarities and differences between Shaw's devil and Bridie's. Now there is no doubt that *Mr Bolfry* owes much of its *vis comica* to the wit and intellectual vigour of Bolfry as demonstrated in its middle movement. Bridie succeeds in making his devil attractive and stimulating, and in making him more of a personality in the theatrical sense than any of the other figures in the play apart from the McCrimmons. Moreover Bolfry is important because he postulates dynamically the central thesis of the play—the Universe as a pattern of the reciprocating opposites of Good and Evil. Yet to throw emphasis on Bolfry at the expense of other aspects and characters is to distort the vision of the whole play and to ignore the fundamental importance of the minister and the Scottish brand of puritanism he represents.

Ursula Gerber refers to Mr Bolfry as McCrimmon's *doppelgänger;* and from the text we observe how frequently Bridie emphasises the idea of Bolfry as McCrimmon's *alter ego.* I believe that Bridie is here concerned most of all with giving us a portrait, a dramatic portrait, of a Scottish Presbyterian minister with the Devil as an important part of the portrait. McCrimmon provides the intellectual dynamism of the first movement of the play: the first climax of the debate between the Minister and the young agnostics is not only a good illustration of Bridie's conception of the drama as argument, but it is also the first full-length view of McCrimmon as chief protagonist—McCrimmon at the height of his intellectual powers. A good portrait should however be concerned with the inner workings of the *psyche* as well as with the outward appearance and the workings of the intelligence. What we have in the metaphysical core of the play is the other side of McCrimmon—the side conjured out of hell. This is the more striking theatrically for being presented as another person—as Bealphares or Bolfry, a Devil.

This *alter ego* theme is visually exploited in *Mr Bolfry* just as the curtain comes down at the end of the second scene, as Minister and Devil are exchanging civilities; and it is expressed explicitly in words in McCrimmon's bursts of soul-searching—mostly in the third scene but also in the final scene. In the developing pace of the play in the third scene, the conflict within McCrimmon is expressed by means of the argument between Minister and Devil, and, what is perhaps more unexpected and striking, McCrimmon's intellectual power and his strong sense of the spiritual are illustrated by the alliance of Minister and Devil as they try to convince the young people that they *have* souls to battle for. The emotional aspect of the character study is filled out in the physical reactions of the Minister to the Devil's call for the loosening of all restraints, and later in the reported violence off-stage on the moor. Two further stages in the portrait are etched in. When McCrimmon returns from the chase we have a glimpse of the dissolute divinity student he had been and an impression of the humbler person he has become. In the final scene the portrait is completed: McCrimmon has reached a state of grace; he has fought the devil within him, recognised his weaknesses and overcome them, admits his pride and returns to the spiritual force he had neglected—his Faith. It is a portrait of a particular minister in the West Highlands at a particular period in history, but it has a universal application. Within each minister of the Gospel, within each person of high moral and religious principles, lies the devil that has to be mastered. The principle of reciprocating opposites applies to the individual as well as to the universe.

All this is made explicit by Bridie in his dialogue and by means of his theatrical technique. Helen L. Luyben complains that it is made too explicit: she says there is nothing here of the subtlety to be found in *The Switchback,* which deals with a similar theme. It is true the themes and character qualities of *Mr Bolfry* are made explicit, but this is not to say that the play is a superficial document which merely states the obvious and the conventional. On the contrary, the obvious and the conventional, in the form of the young people's agnosticism and shallow thinking, are exposed mercilessly in the light of the arguments set forth by McCrimmon and his *alter ego*. One of the most stimulating moments in the play occurs in Scene III when Bolfry leagues himself with McCrimmon in showing up the specious reasoning of the young people and in challenging their assertions about the non-existence of the soul.

All the same, I am not at all sure that everything in the play *is* made explicit. A case is made out by Bolfry for the principle of reciprocating opposites; and later it is made clear that the Devil has been exorcised by McCrimmon and by what might be called the umbrella trick. McCrimmon's last words are about faith; and he himself seems a greatly subdued man by the end. Although there has been a resolution of a kind, there remain the postulation and the illustrations of the reciprocating opposites of Good and Evil. Mrs McCrimmon's final speech brings together two opposites of a different kind—the natural and the supernatural, the physical and the metaphysical, tea and the "queer things that happen in the Bible". By juxtaposing these opposites, the ending neatly epitomises the dual nature of the play; but it also subtly hints at one of its main motifs—the limitations of understanding. I shall return to this final speech later.

Mrs McCrimmon, "the key to the whole business", is an elusive character to deal with. She represents at the beginning the link with common humanity and physical comfort. In the first part of the play she participates in a dialogue with Cohen that is banal in the extreme. James Agate made the point that the play only became adult when "Mr Bridie's devil comes in". I feel the play "lifts" earlier—when McCrimmon comes in and we have the first rise to the debate in Scene I. There is a temptation too in dealing with the achievement of *Mr Bolfry* to praise the "storm centre"—the scene with the Devil—at the expense of the rest of the drama. There is also danger in judging Mrs McCrimmon too readily on first impressions. Here Mrs Bannister's comments turn out in retrospect to be illuminating. She says on the one hand that Mrs McCrimmon as housewife is "a stock Bridie part", but on the other she admits "somehow the part comes up fresh each time it is played by an experienced actress". The important thing about Mrs McCrimmon is not whether or not she is stock Bridie: it is rather that Bridie weaves the part closely into the fabric of the play and in doing so extends the scope of the character. Mrs McCrimmon is not merely a housewife and representative of domestic order: she is also the *punctum indifferens*, the distancing agent, the catalyst. She reduces the emotional atmosphere at the height of the supernatural storm; and she sets her

70

husband's experiences with the Devil in perspective by presenting them in a homely Scots idiom and context.

By comparison the young people tend to be shown up in all their brittle superficiality. They start by being the discontented ones, the challengers: it is they who take the initiative in calling up the Devil from his "extremely comfortable quarters". Jean shows a certain fearless delight in challenging both McCrimmon and the Devil; but intellectually she is no match for either. Her ideas on religion ("The Kingdom of God is within me") are the hackneyed ones of the would-be intellectual. Cohen is precisely what Bolfry said he was—comic relief. Indeed, in creating Cohen, Bridie shows his skill in writing humorous lines designed to put an audience in a relaxed receptive mood. Cully is a more subtle character: his is the discontent of the young intellectual capable of putting up a good argument but eventually vanquished by the superior debating powers of Devil and Minister. The entr'acte in which Bolfry tries to find a dramatic pattern for the two couples is a commentary on their lack of purpose and ineffectiveness as human creatures:

> Perhaps that's what's wrong with you young people. You don't seem to have any pattern.

It is this lack of pattern that shows up so obviously in the debate with McCrimmon and Bolfry, and results in the defeat of the young people. In the end Bridie seems to lose interest in the quartet. The peripheral, formal part they play in the finale is in significant contrast to the action they initiate at the beginning.

If we are inclined to feel a little impatient with the earlier scenes of *Mr Bolfry* because of their conventional clichéd tone, we should remember that these serve to throw the great debate and its sequel into high relief.

71

Certainly the language of these earlier sequences is thin and commonplace—just as Pinter's language deliberately reflects the inanities of conversation. But there is a careful build-up to the first debating climax; and from there the rise to the supernatural core is steady and well-paced. All this is accompanied by a change in the style of language. From the thin phatic West End dialogue we move to the more measured words of McCrimmon, sometimes pompous, frequently enriched with echoes from the Authorised Version. The great debate in the heart of the play has considerable rhetorical power, sometimes veering towards the lush and the florid, sometimes intermingled with the earthy and conversational. We find interesting contrasts too between McCrimmon at his most priestly and pompous, and McCrimmon chastened by his experiences with the Devil. In his final speeches there is a quiet direct quality that isolates and throws into relief important moral statements: "We've a thing called Faith in us"; "I was over proud of my head".

Bridie's Devil Scene in *Mr Bolfry* has affinities with Shaw's Hell Scene in *Man and Superman*. Both devils display great wit; but Bridie's devil is a much less glib, more human kind of intellectual than Shaw's. The debate in *Mr Bolfry* is not so wide ranging as the debate in *Man and Superman*; but Bridie gains in concentration and humanity. There is an important difference in the concluding scenes too: John Tanner seems to have been little affected by the dream-experience in Hell—he talks as freely as ever, whereas the visitation of the Devil has clearly had a profound effect on McCrimmon—his talk is more subdued. Indeed there are moments when the Bridie play becomes a serious study of a human soul passing through an agonising experience, moments when we discern in *Mr Bolfry* an impression of *King Lear*. But the switching from the natural to the supernatural and back, from the homely to the metaphysical and back, and the setting of the banal and the conventional alongside the moral, religious and dialectic—this kind of oscillation or juxtaposition gives the play its essentially comic quality.

This quality is reflected in the overall structure and design into which the portrait of McCrimmon is firmly integrated. *Mr Bolfry* is described as "a play in four scenes", and is set in "a parlour in the Free Kirk Manse at Larach, in the West Highlands of Scotland". Despite the mechanical division into four parts marked by curtain drops, the play seems to be patterned dramatically in three movements. The first begins at a mundane level, rises to its first dialectic climax—the argument between the Minister and the young people—and ends with the intellectual triumph of the Minister. The second movement builds up to the melodramatic-metaphysical core of the play—the debate between the Minister and the Devil— presented in two parts and ending with the flight over the moor and the return of McCrimmon demoralised. The last movement completes the change in McCrimmon: by the end he has turned away from pride in his intellect back to his faith; and the play ends with a humorous return to the supernatural motif in the miraculous exit of Bolfry's umbrella. The progress of the play then is from a very down-to-earth naturalistic opening to a highly meta-physical timeless centre and back to an uncertain naturalism disturbed by the final fling of the supernatural at the end.

I conclude with a study of the finale (Scene IV) to see how far it clarifies and illuminates the central theme and restores comic perspective to the play. Here we return to the domestic realism of the morning after. The bright sunshine mentioned in the stage direction and the cheerful talk of herrings for breakfast form a contrast to the dark supernatural happenings. The only indication that something untoward has happened lies in Mrs

73

McCrimmon's news that the minister has had a disturbed night. The second sequence begins formally—with McCrimmon's entry, his blessing, and the references to the storm. All seems calm and in order. It is only when the dialogue concentrates on the minister and Jean that we have the emotional passage in which the fantasy is pieced together again in terms of McCrimmon's whisky drinking and the "whirling vision" he has had of himself—

... disputing with Beelzebub himself in this very room and racing over the moor with a knife in my hand.

This second sequence of the final scene contains an explicit statement about the central themes of the whole play. Here we have in McCrimmon's at times comic, at times serious, recapitulation of the story of his struggle with Bolfry not only a confession about "the queer dark corners . . . and the strange beasts" in his mind, not only a clear reference to the *alter ego* explanation ("It was my own mind speaking") but also the moral lesson in universal and personal terms. He has returned to the faith he had neglected and he feels its essential importance:

We've a thing called Faith in us, Jean; and we've no more command over it than we have over our lungs.

This is the general truth he has relearned; but the personal lesson is also there, explicitly expressed in a brief sentence near the end of his speech. McCrimmon is the protagonist who has been brought low by his particular form of *hubris:*

I was over proud of my head.

The off-stage episode of the fantasy—the chase over the

moor and the driving of Bolfry into the sea—is seen as the sequel to the debate and the symbolic triumph of Good over Evil:

> But in the middle of all the talk it (his faith) rose up within me and told me to strike the Devil dead . . . in my delirium, mind you.

The last sequence brings together all the characters except Morag for the final commentary and resolution. In seeking for an explanation for the strange experiences that were shared by all, the dialogue throws up ideas of mass hypnotism before it focuses dramatically on the room itself—the setting where they seem to have taken place:

> *McCrimmon.* It is a peaceful room. Everything is natural. Everything obeys the laws of nature. It is the sign of a . . . let me see . . . it is the sign of a supernatural event that everything obeys the laws of nature except one thing . . .

This concentration on the physical setting prepares us for the little metaphysical happening within that setting that is to exorcise the spirit of Bolfry:

> *All look towards the umbrella on the hearth. There is a tense pause. Then the umbrella gets up and walks by itself out of the room.*

Mrs McCrimmon again shows herself to be the guiding spirit. She it is who restores comic balance to the play and presents the story from a practical viewpoint—essentially Scottish in its homely treatment of the de'il—that helps to earth the experience and distance the central message:

> Well, well, it seems you had a kind of tuilzie with the
> De'il after all. You're not the first good and godly man
> who did the like of that . . .

At the end, the two planes on which the play has
operated—the mundane and the metaphysical—are set
alongside each other in Mrs McCrimmon's concluding
speech in which we reach a resolution and attain a sense of
proportion:

> Drink up your tea . . . Och, well, dear me, a walking
> umbrella is nothing to the queer things that happen in the
> Bible. Whirling fiery wheels and all these big beasts
> with the three heads and horns. It's very lucky we are
> that it was no worse. Drink up your tea.

Mrs McCrimmon has become the key to the situation in
the sense that she can by her matter-of-fact attitude and
homely words distance the metaphysical happenings and
place them in their biblical and domestic contexts.

Mr Gillie (1950) is an important Bridie play because the
author has put so much of himself and his "philosophy"
into the chief character. This has been noted and elaborated
by Gabriel Marcel who believed that here Bridie has
formulated the kind of credo that best expresses his own
attitude to his life and art. At the end of his article M.
Marcel said we must be grateful to Bridie for having in this
play proclaimed, at a time when bureaucracy in socially
advanced countries was tending to smother life, the rights
of the individual and the creative urge ("Les droits
imprescriptibles de la personne et de l'effort créateur").
Ursula Gerber also thinks we may assume a close
connection between the author and the character of Gillie.
She says that Bridie bestowed on his character his own

personal artistic credo ("seinen persönlichen künstlerischen Credo"). It is important to stress this credo from the outset. Throughout the play, and in contrast to the meannesses and opportunism that surround him, Gillie extols and exemplifies *enthousiasmos,* the god-given zeal of the artist. It is this quality that gives the play its drive and energy, and therefore affects its dramatic pattern.

The play is important too for its sharp criticism of man and society. As in *Dr Angelus* so in *Mr Gillie*, Bridie reveals the insensitivity and cruelty that lie behind hypocrisy and sentimentality. In particular Gibb and Watson, clergyman and doctor, are sharply satirised for their middle-class complacency which is exposed with a relish that would appeal to Jimmy Porter. The portrayal of the sordid life of amoral opportunism lived by Tom and Nelly in London amongst the petty journalists, manipu-lators and film men is an example of Bridie's social realism. It is an impression of the kind of background that was to be satirised in the novels, plays, films, and TV documentaries of the fifties and later. This facing up to reality—to the sordid, the immoral, the criminal—was no new thing for Bridie: *The Anatomist* and *A Sleeping Clergyman* emerge from or plunge into sordid surround-ings and derive some of their dynamic power from sordid acts. The new note struck in *Mr Gillie* is the persistence of the sordid: if anything the atmosphere is darker at the end than at the beginning, for Gillie is surrounded by examples of treachery, hypocrisy, cheap success founded on cynical opportunism and the worship of money. The dialogue echoes with hollow clichés and thin contemporary colloquialisms that catch the spirit of the time just as Pinter's dialogue was to catch the lifelessness, the lack of spirit or individuality in his characters less than a decade later.

The play may also be regarded as an attack on conventional education and educational thinking of the time. Tom Donnelly's criticism of Gillie's schoolmasterly tendencies—the recourse to the tawse, the authoritarianism, the old-fashioned belief in Milton, Browning, Carlyle and Ruskin—may or may not still be valid; but the sharp criticism of educational attitudes that comes from Gillie himself at climactic points in the play remains relevant. Gillie's is not a criticism of education or books or literature: it is rather a cry for freedom, freedom from the repressions of the classroom and the restrictions of community life, from the domination of Civil Service and Parliament. Gillie's rebellion against the education authority and against Gibb its representative comes from a deep-rooted feeling *against* convention and restriction and *for* the creative power of life manifested by artists of all kinds. It springs from his *enthousiasmos*, his zeal to express himself and to encourage self-expression and self-fulfilment in others.

The play concentrates its dramatic power on Gillie. It is Gillie who gives it shape and pace; it is Gillie who is at its heart and round whom the other characters rotate. Mrs Gillie is a mere domestic influence on the periphery, encouraging or soothing or scolding her husband as if he were a child: she is a stock character—a variant of the housewife or the shrew—used deliberately. Watson is a satirical portrait of a self-indulgent, mean, sentimental professional man: his function is to emphasise Gillie's integrity. In himself he is a kind of spluttering *pantalone*. Gibb is the conventional man of religion—glib, dictatorial, shallow, but not merely the Priest or Pedant of the *commedia dell' arte* tradition. He also represents the unimaginative public servant mouthing clichés. As for the apparently talented couple Tom and Nelly, the lovers who break their pattern, Bridie makes his sharpest commentary on society as it was developing in the postwar period of the late forties by showing how easily a man-woman relationship can become distorted and destroyed when brought into contact with the corruptions of a big city.

The play is essentially what its title suggests—a character drama, a portrait of Mr Gillie schoolmaster. In the first part we see him teaching his pupil with characteristic zest; we see him treating Dr Watson with the humanity Watson does not deserve; and we see him defying convention to encourage youth—his promising ex-pupils Tom, a young miner, and Nelly, Watson's daughter. The quality that seems to make him less than human— his detachment—in reality serves to isolate him from his fellows and make him stand out as a character, as a person of spirit, a person possessed by a spirit. The second part of the play depicting the return of Tom and Nelly from London brings about the wreck of his hopes: his optimism and belief in the couple have proved ill-founded. This again gives Bridie an opportunity to develop the character study and show the subtleties of Gillie's *psyche*. At a time when doctor and priest are praising the couple for being successful, for "making good" (meaning making money) in London, he has the clear sight and the honesty to admit his mistake, to denounce the pose of success, and reveal it as the failure of spirit that it really is.

According to one kind of dramatic pattern, Gillie would have become a figure of remorse at the end. He would have been seen to have come through the fire and the agony, having suffered from his mistakes and become contrite. According to another kind of pattern, he would have been seen to have been affected by the corruption, and would go off to the party reconciled to the group. It is a sign of Bridie's originality that he does not end his play in either of these ways. Gillie's belief in the artist remains intact, his enthusiasm for the artistic life unimpaired: it is this credo that enables him to resist absorption in the group and distances him from his own troubles. *Mr Gillie* as a play has therefore a shape and a method of its own. It does not conform to the pattern of tragedy or tragi-comedy. Although it is strongly satirical it does not conform to the pattern of satirical comedy or absurdist drama with a perfunctory or negative conclusion. It is part of Bridie's comic pattern that his main character should be seen at the end still believing in his theory and his *métier*—the theory of the artist as someone to be encouraged and cherished, and his *métier* as true teacher—stimulator and encourager of the latent talents of the young.

All this is vividly illustrated in the final sequence where a kind of family reunion is staged. First Watson then Nelly comes in to take part in a false reconciliation act which begins with a comic ritual of shaking hands. Watson has already posed as outraged father, betrayed friend, hard-working doctor, and magnanimous father welcoming back the prodigal daughter. Now in putting on a *nunc dimittis* act, he presents another parody:

Here's me toiling and moiling all these years with no other idea in the world but to get Nelly nicely settled and married to a decent young fellow that could make his way. And now the dearest wish of my heart has been fulfilled. Now lettest thou thy servant depart in peace.

As this final sequence draws to a close, Bridie by throwing out a reference to another promising pupil prepares us for a return to the main theme of the play. Mary McLeish, a talented girl, will probably have to give up drawing lessons because of family misfortunes. Gillie accepts the gift of a drawing of Nelly by Mary which then begins to stir new visions in his mind. In the coda to this final act the commentary by husband and wife on the events just witnessed is made perfunctory so that attention may focus on Gillie's *enthousiasmos* and its new outlet. The picture of Nelly by Mary McLeish provides an opportunity to look back and to look forward, to look from an object of promise unfulfilled to an object of new hope:

Mrs Gillie. It's awful like her.
Mr Gillie. I'm afraid so.
Mrs Gillie. She's not one of your successes.
Mr Gillie. Perhaps not . . . This is a brilliant bit of drawing.

Suddenly the whole story of Tom and Nelly shrinks in importance: it is seen only as a mistake, an experiment gone wrong. One can always start afresh:

Mr Gillie. I'm not Tom's keeper, he can look after himself. He's proved that anyway. I've done no harm, if I've done no good. I was only wrong. There's nothing final about making mistakes—if there's no real harm done. There are more good pit boys where he came from.

By the end of the coda we are back at the beginning again. Gillie sees a touch of original genius about this Mary McLeish—all she needs is encouragement. We return to the idea of a genius as someone possessed:

I'll raise the De'il in her tomorrow.

The last view we have of Gillie illustrates his questing spirit and his belief in the creative urge.

The fantasy-frame, which might at first appear to be mere theatrical decoration, turns out to be the device that puts the whole play into perspective. Too much social realism, too much close naturalism, would tend to blur the edges of truth and make us lose true focus. It is not enough to let a character speak for himself: sometimes he hardly understands himself in any case; and often he is only dimly aware of the pattern he is tracing in life. We see Gillie work out and live up to a credo—a belief in the positive qualities of life: he is completely conscious of the pattern in his *credo*. It is the function of the Chorus—particularly the Judge—to trace the pattern in his *character* and *life*, of which Gillie himself cannot be fully conscious. The strictly legalistic person like the Procurator might well label him a failure and consign him to limbo, but this would come dangerously near to being the logical converse of labelling Tom and Nelly "successes". In talking about the *few moments* of liberation between the cage and the cat, and in talking of honouring the *forlorn hope*, the Judge himself seems to be diminishing the effort and *enthousiasmos* of Gillie; but the significant thing is that he *is* granted his immortality and a place between Lincoln and John Wesley. Watching these fantasy-chorus scenes we may be amused by the mere theatrical magic of it all; but the device as exploited by Bridie is not used merely to delight us and distance the theme, release us from the emotional stress: it also helps us to interpret Gillie, to see the significance of his *credo* and so judge him on a broadly universal rather than a narrow moral basis.

This supernatural device is used outside the main realist action of the play. Within its naturalistic core, however, Bridie exploits another device to stress the thematic viewpoint. It is by the use of irony that Gillie is able to distance himself from his problem. Irony is the weapon he defends himself with—against Gibb, Tom, his wife, Watson. Irony is also the means whereby we as audience are able to anticipate the heavenly judgment that is made on Gillie at the end. We become aware of the ironical contrast between Gillie's hopes for Tom and Nelly and the reality of their sordid adventures in London, between the examples of Gillie's failures and his continuing belief in the artistic vision. *Mr Gillie* may be regarded as a satire in that the hypocrisies and pretensions and meannesses of life are revealed in all their nakedness. But it may also be regarded as something more positive—a comedy which illustrates the romance of hope and idealism. It is a romantic comedy of a special kind. The final impression is not the power of its satire great though that is. It may not even be the balanced judgment that emerges from the fantasy-frame. It may rather be the impression of Gillie's *credo.* Despite the emotionalism and harsh criticism of society, it is the power of Gillie's optimism that lingers after the play has been read or viewed in performance.

It remains true however that at the core of *Mr Gillie* there lies a dilemma of modern life—the contradiction between the growing dishonesty and cheapening of life on the one hand and its great possibilities on the other. In writing this play Bridie was as concerned with attacking hypocrisy and narrow morality as John Osborne was in writing *Look Back in Anger* in 1956. Both *Mr Gillie* and *Look Back in Anger* reflect the malaise in society of the post-war era; but whereas Osborne was concerned with the problem of class barriers, snobbery, the plight of the educated working-class person stranded in bourgeois territory, Bridie was concerned with the problem of spiritual and moral barriers, the plight of an enlightened person who saw his work of encouraging and inspiring the young frustrated by opportunism and selfishness in the classless jungle of postwar society. The difference is an important one and can be traced to Bridie's Scottish background. Gillie is concerned with shaking himself free from the prejudices and petty restrictions of society as a whole; Porter is concerned with shaking himself free of class prejudices. Bridie is attacking meanness in all strata of society; Osborne's target is middle-class morality. Osborne's title is significant: his play seems at times to be looking back with nostalgia not at a classless age but at the Edwardian age with its superficial courtesy and elegance. Bridie is not looking back at all; nor is his main character angry except on rare occasions. The achievement of *Mr Gillie* is that it presents the postwar era in all its sordidness and malaise and yet succeeds in being forward-looking. At the end, Gillie begins again to experiment creatively with art and with promising pupils: he looks forward in zest.

The verdict on Gillie's life given in the Epilogue stresses this optimism and further releases us from the narrow preoccupations of social realism. The Judge in awarding Gillie his place among the immortals between Lincoln and John Wesley not only adds a comic detachment to the play but also indicates its universality. Lincoln would have welcomed a fellow liberator; Wesley would have recognised that Gillie's code was grounded on his own faith, and would have welcomed Gillie as one who laboured faithfully in his vocation. In the end we are impressed by the urbanity and the sanity of divine justice hovering over this Epilogue. The urbanity releases us from concern with Gillie as a person; the sanity of divine judgment in commending Gillie, in seeing in his life "a kind of success" (as James Michie noted in his article), appeals strongly to us examining the matter *sub specie aeternitatis.*

Both *Mr Bolfry* and *Mr Gillie* derive their dramatic strength and shape from the dynamic qualities of their central figures. The central figure is frequently the object of criticism and even hostility: McCrimmon antagonises Jean and her friends; Gillie is frequently isolated from the group—from his wife, pupils, Watson, Gibb. But more important than any physical isolation is the intellectual isolation. These are characters whose intellectual and moral ideas mark them off from the minor figures who surround them. McCrimmon delights in intellectual conflict: he is "over proud" of his head. Gillie may not be well endowed with creative gifts, nor does he have great powers of judgment; but his intellectual superiority is evident in his dealings with pupil, doctor and minister.

One interesting difference between the two portraits is illustrated by the endings. Gillie is off to a new beginning, still believing in his mission to encourage talent and still believing in the supremacy of the creative urge. McCrimmon is not so sure of himself at the end: indeed so deeply has he been affected by his experience that he is content to let the initiative pass to his wife. The portrait of McCrimmon is perhaps the more complete one: by the device of the *alter ego* we have a view into his *psyche* as well as his mind; and we see him pass through the stages of the classical hero from pride to humility. Gillie seems at times too much abstracted, too impersonal to allow himself full expression; yet the sardonic detached quality that emerges in certain sequences is just as important in summing up Gillie as his enthusiasm for art and his fierce desire for freedom. If McCrimmon's is the more complete portrait, Gillie's is the subtler.

In both plays the main character stands out not just because he is superior mentally and morally, but also because the other characters are so superficial or corrupt or so manifestly lacking in integrity. *Mr Bolfry* illustrates the mental posing and the lack of intellectual resilience on the part of the young group opposed to McCrimmon; *Mr Gillie* illustrates the decadence or moral dishonesty of the promising or the powerful. In the second we have the sharper indictment of society. Whereas McCrimmon at the end seems to lose something of his originality in gaining humility and insight, Gillie retains his individuality and remains isolated in his beliefs. Yet the result in each case is a dramatic character study subtly developed or still developing. In both plays the accent remains on the central figure. The tendency to relegate supporting characters to the role of chorus is illustrated in the second part of *Mr Gillie,* and in the third and fourth scenes of *Mr Bolfry.*

Both are basically realist dramas that modulate into or out of supernatural sequences; and this movement from one plane to another proves to be an important structural element. The "portraits" are the more revealing for being subjected to the tests of metaphysics or fantasy. In *Mr Bolfry* it is the subconscious of McCrimmon that is explored by the fantasy; in *Mr Gillie* it is the endeavour and inner dynamic of Gillie that are illuminated by the comments of the supernatural figures.

These dramatic portraits turn out to be also amongst the most Scottish of Bridie's plays. It is not merely that he is dealing with the favourite subjects of Scotsmen—religion and education. The Scottish quality comes out in *Mr Bolfry* in the intellectual way the minister presents his beliefs and attitudes, and in *Mr Gillie* in the characteristic combination of detachment and idealism on the part of the educationist. Both illustrate a typically Scottish intensity in moral and intellectual attitudes. Linguistically too these plays have a Scottish colouring. In *Mr Bolfry* this can be traced in the expressions, syntax and vocabulary of the McCrimmons in particular. Gillie's speech is little affected by Scots: in this respect he may be regarded as a fairly typical Scottish schoolmaster; but the language of Watson and Mrs Gillie has at times a flavour of traditional Scots in turn of phrase and vocabulary.

One important point to be noted about these plays is that Bridie is not restricting Scots to the servant or lower classes. He is rather demonstrating the Scots element still to be found in the speech of the Scottish professional classes; and this is linked with his Scottish attitude towards the problem of class consciousness. It is not that class distinctions are unknown in Scotland: we have our own problems of snobbery linguistic and social; but there is a deep-rooted tendency amongst Scots to ignore class barriers and accents and judge a man for what he is. Bridie in these plays deals with educational, social and intellectual questions from the viewpoint of society as a whole. He attacks the narrowmindedness of the Community and the Civil Service, or the immaturity of youth "educated" and "uneducated" alike, not class prejudices or merely middle-class morality.

CHAPTER FOUR

Two "Poetic" Experimental Plays

FROM TIME TO TIME throughout his career but particularly in his later period Bridie seems to have been interested in applying certain themes and characters in myths, legends, classical stories to contemporary situations. As far back as 1938 in *The Babes in the Wood* he uses as ground bass the Faustus legend—Goethe's version of it rather than Marlowe's. Robert Gillet, the schoolmaster who has written a best-seller, comes under the spell of his Mephistopheles—Brewer the publisher. Like Peer Gynt, however, Gillet is saved from damnation by the love of a good wife. *The Queen's Comedy* (1950) is a retelling of a story from the fourteenth and fifteenth books of the *Iliad* of the gods and mortals involved in the Trojan War. The parallel between the lot of the twentieth-century soldier and that of his ancient prototype is vividly suggested in Bridie's use of sub-standard colloquial dialect; but the most powerful dramatic moments emerge from non-naturalistic sequences—the dead Greek soldier's attack on the amorality of the gods and Jupiter's concluding account of his experiment with life.

In two plays in particular, it seems to me, Bridie has effectively interwoven the contemporary with the legendary or mythological. In *Daphne Laureola* he draws out of the story of a young Pole's obsession for an older woman a parallel with the story of Apollo's obsession with the nymph Daphne who was transformed by Gaea into a laurel bush before she could be possessed. This play remains rooted in its naturalistic settings throughout its three movements; but, restricted though he is by this, Bridie contrives to modulate skilfully between the realist and the mythological planes. *The Baikie Charivari* represents Bridie's final attempt to match legend, myth, and Morality with a contemporary situation. His story of Sir James Pounce-Pellott, ex-governor of an Indian district, come home to Baikie to learn the new ways of postwar Scotland, is told naturalistically and surrealistically. The play moves from one plane to the other sometimes gradually sometimes suddenly; and here Bridie is at his boldest in using "poetic" and widely varied linguistic styles. Both *Daphne Laureola* and *The Baikie Charivari* use some of the devices of poetic drama— intensification by the introduction of metaphorical or allegorical parallels, modulation to non-realist planes, the interweaving of myth with contemporary story.

Opinion seems to be divided about the success of the first of these "poetic" experimental plays—*Daphne Laureola* (1949). It is for some people too complicated in its use of symbolism and in its references to its central myth. At the time of its first production in America in 1950 New York critics complained of the "fuzzy and unnecessary symbolism" and the over-burdening of the plot "with mythological allusions . . . and quasi-poetical declamations", to quote from an article by Walter Kerr in *The Commonweal* and from another in *Theatre Arts.* On the other hand, British critics seem to have been impressed by its power and insight. Harold Hobson thought the first act "extremely striking", and praised the characterisation of "Lady Pitts's very old, calm husband"; and Eric Linklater described *Daphne Laureola* as "a play of profound insight, of a broad and human poetic quality".

One of the most striking features of this play is the detailed characterisation of Lady Pitts; and of Bridie critics Ursula Gerber seems to be the most appreciative in praising Bridie's skill and success here in building up his portrait of a lady: "Hier ist Bridie gelungen, das Porträt einer zentralen Figur zu schaffen . . . " Winifred Bannister deals with the ordinary characters—the "pedestrians" as she calls them, and finds them "off the peg", not particularly well drawn. We have to remember, however, the practice of Greek classical theatre in exploiting figures who comment and unfold their restricted or extended viewpoint in order to throw into high relief the main action and the main characters. Bridie's use of the spivs, the couples, Gooch and Watson, suggests a parallel with classical choric technique and a concern with form and theme rather than the conventional preoccupation with minor character study. The figure of George the waiter is sufficiently shadowy and peripheral to be regarded as a choric character too: he reminds us at times of Shaw's waiter in *You Never Can Tell,* particularly in the way he helps to earth the emotional exchanges by his deferential talk. The three men who surround Lady Pitts are delineated in more detail—Ernest courteous, passionate, 'poetic'; Sir Joseph wise, testy, sardonic; Vincent watchful, opportunist, crude. They represent types of suitors to Lady Pitts—the poet, the rich old man, the jealous watchdog. The real significance of Lady Pitts's choice of Vincent rather than Ernest becomes clear only if we regard the suitors as types: carefully individualised characters would tell us relatively nothing. Lady Pitts comes to prefer the watchdog because he makes smaller demands on her soul.

But all these characters—choric, stock or individu-alised—remain subservient to the main figure. Lady Pitts is the emancipated woman, the blue stocking, the misfit, the kept woman, the young wife of an old man. She is *femina sapiens*, the brilliant Newnham graduate, the female intellectual who has been unable to steer a course through life and has begun to disintegrate. She may be

Bridie's version of the kind of woman Ibsen had dealt with. A Nora out of her *Doll's House* might have had to face such failure as a free woman; a Hedda Gabler rejecting suicide might have been driven to similar negative decisions. The compromise reached by Ellida in rejecting her Stranger from the Sea and remaining with her husband is not unlike that reached by Lady Pitts in marrying Vincent: both choose a kind of emancipation from romance. Yet we must not make the mistake of assuming that the realist version of her character—her own version basically— is the truth. Ernest sees her as a goddess—remote, unattainable, but fascinating, desirable, adorable. She has an ethereal quality that suggests contact with things other than the earthy. In her unguarded moments she yearns for adventure, rejects conventional attitudes, even longs for Ernest as her lover. There is a third side to her nature: she is the civilised domestic female, solicitous and loving towards her husband, orderly and organising, stage-managing, civil, hospitable. It is highly significant that the structure of the play reflects the different and contrasting aspects of her nature. In the first and final acts she reveals her challenging, unorthodox, Cassandra-like wisdom, uninhibited in her drunken or emotional state. In these acts she is the intellectual who oscillates between realism and romanticism. In the middle movement, in the orderly atmosphere of the suburban garden, she is Candida-Nora—domesticated, wise, sweet, feminine. The structure brings out not so much the different sides of an individual woman character as the dilemma, the suffering of any woman who has been emancipated by her intelligence and contaminated by higher education. So far the symbolism of the myth and the insecure flooring of the restaurant has not had to be considered in assessing the power of the dramatic portrait of the central figure in the play.

It is the relationship between Lady Pitts and Ernest

Piaste that is illuminated, given an extra dimension, by the application of the Daphne-Apollo myth. It seems reasonable to assume that this was Bridie's aim in weaving it into the fabric of this play. At first sight the myth seems scarcely appropriate. Daphne was the nymph in classical mythology who was beloved of Apollo but fled from him and was changed by the aged earth-goddess Gaea into a laurel or bay tree before Apollo could seize her. Ernest seems at first too courteous, too passive to fit the rôle of Apollo, and Lady Pitts too mature to play the nymph. But in so far as Ernest's love develops strongly in the middle part of the play, and in so far as he is persuaded to give up the chase by the aged husband, deciding to worship her from afar and perhaps recognising that she has already withdrawn from life under Sir Joseph's glass case, the myth helps to explain and elaborate Ernest's attitude to Lady Pitts and their relationship. The laurel tree planted by Lady Pitts outside the summerhouse at the wrong time of the year is Bridie's theatrical representation of the myth. Lady Pitts feels its importance; Ernest addresses it as Apollo would have addressed the original laurel that had been Daphne. The application of the myth to the love story implies Lady Pitts's removal from active life, her remaining something pure and beautiful in nature; and it also implies that Ernest even remotely will be able to watch her and comfort her. It is ironical that Ernest in his inebriate vision at the end should still see himself as Apollo although his Daphne has taken herself out of Sir Joseph's glass case and sought the protection of the earthy Vincent. Certainly Ernest as poet must continue his "lonely predestinate course, day and night"; and it is to be presumed that it is through the warmth of memory and reflection that Ernest-Apollo is to keep in touch with the lady. It is Ernest's vision of Lady Pitts that the myth stresses—her ethereality, her remoteness, her spiritual quality.

The insecure flooring of the restaurant as symbol fits into the central myth only indirectly. It can be seen to emphasise the instability of contemporary postwar society, Lady Pitts's own insecurity, and the insecurity of Ernest's physical world; but these have little direct bearing on the love affair and the Daphne story. The symbol however has significance in pointing character development or revelation. Lady Pitts's other-worldly quality is illustrated by her safely crossing the floor in the first act; and equally her succumbing to the earthy later is marked by her keeping to the edge with the others when she exits in the final scene.

One thing Bridie does successfully in this play is to present the ethereal and the earthy side by side. At one point Ernest represents the idealist and the pure where Lady Pitts is seen longing for action and the practical experiences of life. Within Lady Pitts herself two tendencies strive for mastery: she is the romantic and the goddess in succumbing to Ernest; she is the realist and the human in yielding to Vincent. This antithesis is also reflected in the language used. The colloquial clichéd dialogue of the choric characters contrasts with Ernest's flights of idealism and Lady Pitts's outbursts which are carefully structured and characterised by fine rhythmic power. One may trace here again that Scottish character-istic—the contrasting of the beautiful with the ugly, an illustration of the Caledonian antisyzygy. The other Scottish characteristic that is to be noted is Ernest's presbyterian quality—his seriousness, his religious intensity, his high idealism. These contrast with certain qualities of the other characters—Sir Joseph's urbanity, the glibness and superficiality of the 'chorus'. It would appear to be Ernest's high Scottish seriousness—passionate and moral—from which in the end Lady Pitts recoils.

Yet about Lady Pitts herself there is a quality of the tragical. Her inner self comes to the surface only twice—once when she shows she is attracted to Ernest in the first act, and again in the middle part where she shows affection for her husband. But in her rejection of illusions, in her desire for danger, above all in her acceptance of Vincent as her official keeper, she seems to have given up her inner life and become, as Helen L. Luyben puts it, "a symbol of an exhausted culture". She represents the failure of the intellectual, the *femina sapiens,* as well as a dried-up specimen kept in a glass case, the life having long since departed. In conveying the impression of the death of hope and illusion in her speeches in the first and final acts, Lady Pitts attains almost tragic stature as a Cassandra-like figure; and there is a kind of irony in the way Ernest idealises her as a remote, goddess-like figure, and yet has to watch her depart into ordinary life as the wife of her former chauffeur. When we apply the myth at this point in our understanding of the play, we begin to realise it may be apposite after all. Daphne's tragedy was that she should have escaped from Apollo by becoming rooted and fixed to the earth for ever as a laurel; Lady Pitts's tragedy was that she escaped from Ernest and his illusions and romantic dreams and demands by marrying Vincent and thus destroying her finer qualities and her inner life.

Daphne Laureola is Bridie's great experiment with the poetic method of symbolism. He could have given us, he did to some extent give us, a portrait of an intellectual lady who had lost her way and had to be rescued by men who became her keepers rather than her saviours. But he clearly wanted to say more about her qualities, aspirations, possibilities and influence on others. To give us a glimpse of her other life, her *alter ego*—the goddess, he introduced the character of Ernest and built in the poetic device of the symbol of the Daphne myth. Perhaps his delight in manipulating his symbols led him to overplay his hand; but there is no doubt that he produced a play of considerable subtlety and beauty. He illustrates here too something that he illustrates in other plays like *Mr Gillie* and *The Baikie Charivari*, namely his credo that realism is not enough, that realism has to be enlivened with fancy and poetry and vision if some of the subtler truths of life are to be uncovered. The design of the play, its cyclic structure noted by Helen L. Luyben, the use of ordinary characters as chorus and background to throw the central figures into high relief, and above all the presenting of these central figures on three different planes realist, idealist, mythic— all these features stress the experimental and poetic nature of *Daphne Laureola*.

Does the experiment succeed? A consideration of its basic design and dramatic shape may help us to visualise the power of the play on the stage. It is constructed according to a familiar Bridie formula: four acts or scenes that fall into three movements. It is important to appreciate its cyclic structure from the outset: the first and fourth acts take place in the London restaurant (with exactly the same people—the minor characters and the principals); the middle two acts take place in the Pitts's summerhouse. The public setting of the dilapidated restaurant, dangerous and in need of repair, contrasts with the private setting of the summerhouse, safe and secluded. The mood of the restaurant scenes is passionate, quarrelsome, and marked by the fantasies of drunkenness; that of the garden scene is for the most part intellectual, orderly, civilised.

An examination of the final act in particular reveals the structural and dramatic power of the play, and the whole significance of its mythic basis and "poetic" quality. In this final act, which may also be regarded as the third movement of the whole play, there is a deliberate and conscious return to the pattern and motifs of the opening. The same people are dining at the same restaurant; the bad piece of flooring is still there; and the play picks up the dialogue of the two spivs precisely where it left it— "So I says to him, look, Maurice . . . " The pattern is carefully repeated. We move from Gooch, Watson, and the young couples to the bored couple (and the iteration of their "cold coffee" refrain) before coming to the heart of the play when the dialogue focuses on Ernest as he enters. Ernest's faint on hearing the news of Sir Joseph's death is Bridie's dramatic method of reminding us of the strength of his involvement with Lady Pitts; and his isolation from the group as he recovers is marked by the contempt he expresses for Gooch and his gossip—and its imagery:

Sir, you are an impudent dog; but nothing that you have to say can either offend or distress me. Your words do not affect me one way or another. You might as well spit at the sky.

The dialogue tails away into trivialities deliberately to throw into high relief the entry of Lady Pitts and Vincent as Mr and Mrs Vincent. The moment of recognition brings out the contrast between the woman's resilience and the man's heavy intensity: according to the stage direction— *She smiles radiantly and bows to Ernest. Ernest stares at her.* We have an example here of Bridie's dramatic use of the chorus. Gooch plays the part of chorus-leader congratulating the couple and fatuously leading the group in song. The structure of the play is striking at this point: as the jollifications die away and the dialogue quietly brings Ernest and Lady Pitts together, there comes a gradual rise to the last big "poetic" climax. Ernest's reaction to the marriage with Vincent is sharp to the point of the tragical: it enables him to present his own love for Lady Pitts as a parody of the Daphne myth:

It is a very old story. Has nobody told you the story of the poor peasant who worshipped a goddess? . . . Has nobody told you about the god who loved a mortal girl, thinking she was as he was, and found that she was a no-good slut?

His own vision imaginative and cosmic is now transformed into something loathsome and filthy:

The blessed sun has changed to a huge scorpion and the great mountains to pestiferous dunghills and the green grass to bile.

The play reaches its greatest climax at this point—an inner poetic climax of tremendous intensity and symbolic power. Ernest's religious-romantic *credo* is embellished with a quotation from Dante and echoes from the story of the Creation. His love for Lady Pitts is equated with the beginning of life; and its destruction brings nothing but ruin and desolation:

On the day I first saw you, there came light, day and night came and the stars and the sun and the moon, the ocean and the land filled themselves with life and a man and a woman were born to be king and queen over all. Now all is ruin and desolation for ever and ever.

After the high idealism comes the low realism: Lady Pitts exaggerates the other side of the picture. Such idealist men are merely in love with themselves; they are not even interested in the lies women tell. She comes down in favour of the human pigs—people like Vincent:

And the pigs are at least honest with themselves and with us . . . That's why I've settled down in a nice clean pig-sty.

Even Ernest's fairy story is given a vicious twist to justify her action in marrying Vincent:

> You wanted to save the distressed lady from the ogre, didn't you? But the lady was too old to play these games, and she married the ogre and settled down.

But when the speech is over and there is a return from rhetoric to practical dialogue Lady Pitts becomes apologetic and clear-sighted. Indeed, to both her and Ernest there comes a sudden realisation that they are after all merely mortals manipulated by outside forces, as the moon manipulates the sea:

> *Ernest.* Why should I forgive you? You have done me no wrong. It is not you who have done all this.
> *Lady Pitts.* . . . These things are as old as the moon. The white goddess swings the tides idly to and fro and the little coloured wriggling things in the swaying seas know her . . . Go back into the sea, Ernest. The moon is a silly, cold goddess . . .

Lady Pitts's transformation from cold goddess to ordinary mortal is demonstrated as she walks off stage: this time she takes care to circle the dangerous floor with the others.

In the coda the thematic symbolism of the play bubbles up quietly out of the naturalistic dialogue. What we have now is a mere formal expression of the metaphor out of the mouth of an Ernest bemused by brandy and an exaggerated sense of his own vocation. The picture we had at the beginning of the play of a tipsy Lady Pitts penetrating her romantic illusions is balanced by the picture we have at

the end of Ernest formalising the story of his defeated
hopes and aspirations:

> I am Apollo. She is Daphne. Apollo wanted Daphne
> so much that the old man changed her into a laurel tree.
> But Apollo still rode on his predestined course, day and
> night, day and night.

Both in their different scenes—Lady Pitts at the
beginning, Ernest at the end—drink double brandies. It
seems that Bridie wants us to see both visions—the
debunking of illusions and the formalising of the Daphne
allegory—as opposite aspects of the truth. Throughout,
the structure of the play has juxtaposed the romantic with
the realist, the naturalistic with the symbolic. In presenting
the coarse mundane aspects of Lady Pitts's life and
character alongside Ernest's vision of her as a goddess,
Bridie does seem to be expressing that characteristically
Scottish obsession with the contradictions of life. In this
sense *Daphne Laureola* may be Bridie's dramatic and
symbolic representation of the Caledonian antisyzygy,
"the unique blend of the lyrical and the ludicrous", the
typically Scottish "reconciliation between the base and
the beautiful" as Hugh MacDiarmid defined it in *The
Scottish Chapbook*.

The last play *The Baikie Charivari* (1952) is the most
complex and the most experimental of all Bridie's works;
yet it represents an attempt to go back to simple primitive
aspects of drama, to mediaeval forms, to folklore and
legend, and the biblical sources behind these. Bridie called
it a Miracle Play, a sub-title that emphasises its scriptural
origin. It has behind it the figure of Pontius Pilate, by some
regarded as a betrayer of Christ, by others (for example
the Abyssinian Church) as a saint. The play is aptly

named. Firstly, it is rooted in Scotland: Baikie stands for Scotland; the De'il is a Scottish figure speaking Scots and well aware of the weaknesses of the inhabitants of Baikie, well aware he can hoodwink and manipulate them, knowing they will gladly play their part in trying to bring down Pounce-Pellott the Proud, just as the bodies of Barbie brought down John Gourlay the Proud in *The House with the Green Shutters*. Secondly, despite its complexities, it relies on the simplicities of the legendary story of Punch and Judy for some of its dramatic and symbolic effects. It is a 'charivari' in the sense that it lets us hear the wrangling of the seven 'prophets'; it is a 'charivari' because no harmony comes out of their rough 'serenading' of P-P, and because it contains a strong sense of satire and disapproval. The title must be taken in its ironical sense too: *The Baikie Charivari* reveals not only the noisy ineffectiveness of the seven prophets and their remedies: it also illustrates the unpromising setting, physical and intellectual, within which a governor retired from the East, a Pounce-Pellott, a Pontius Pilate, has to work and strive, preserve and develop his soul to reach a state of grace.

Pounce-Pellott himself seems a complicated figure. At the historical level he represents the British Imperialist governor who has renounced his power after the British withdrawal from India. At the contemporary level he is the ruler who, having imposed order on an alien race, has now come home to face a lack of order and a lack of pattern amongst his own people. He represents the man who has to be re-educated to fit into a new environment, the man who has to have new guides and teachers. Bridie skilfully combines the contemporary with the Morality in dramatising Pounce-Pellott's process of re-education. The teachers are seven contemporary false prophets representing artistic self-indulgence (Joey), religious pomposity and self-esteem (Beadle), the temptations of financial gain (Jemima Lee Crowe), the inefficiency and stupidity of established authority (Copper), authoritarianism in political dogma (Ketch), glib doctrines in psychology (Pothecary), the spent force of outmoded aristocracy (Lady Maggie). The play depicts the hounding, testing and tempting of James Pounce-Pellott by these corrupting forces of modern civilisation who turn out to be the devil's agents intent on destroying his soul. The method used by Bridie to expose the prophets and the dangers of their restricted dogma-ridden philosophies is, as in *Mr Gillie*, that of irony. With an ironical charm Pounce-Pellott engages the prophets to act as his teachers, invites them to the dinner-party-symposium, and encourages them to wrestle for his soul. The ironical quality enables P-P to remain detached for the most part: in this he forms a striking contrast to his wife Judy who is portrayed as being emotionally involved—the harried housewife, the shrew, the conservative reacting against democratic tendencies. Only once does P-P show signs of losing his composure— when he finds Joey attempting to seduce his daughter; and it is important for an understanding of the pattern of the play that we realise the importance of Baby the daughter (whose name is derived from the Punch story). Although she is depicted on the realist plane as shallow, sensualist, self-indulgent, she represents something precious beyond herself, something that has already been saved from death, something that has still to be saved from spiritual evil, something that can develop and grow only in fresh surroundings. Thus although Ketch saved her, she has to be rescued both from the evil of initiation into the Devil's Way in the fantasy and from the evil of Joey's attempted seduction. It is in accordance with the Morality pattern of the play that she should in the end be given to Toby, the young apprentice, uncorrupted by the world's slow stain.

The parallel in *The Tempest* helps to make clear the relationship: Pounce-Pellott all through the play prizes and preserves Baby, as Prospero does Miranda; and he terrifies and therefore in a way tests Toby, as Prospero does Ferdinand.

It is not important in this kind of symbolic play to consider how well or overdrawn any of the characters may be, especially those seven characters who live a double or a treble life in the course of the action. If I were to criticise any one at the naturalistic level I would single out Jemima Lee Crowe who could be considered an overdrawn stock American figure; but I should also have to admit that one of the best scenes in the play is the one in which, as a publisher's agent, she tempts P-P with gold for writing his memoirs of his life in India. What Bridie contrives to do in this play is to fit stock figures from the Punch and Judy legend, figures from the *commedia dell' arte* and mediaeval Morality traditions, into his contemporary story and situation, so as to strengthen the dramatic impact and sharpen the social commentary. His Beadle not only has the egocentric absurdity of the type: he has all the glib hypocrisy, conceit and narrow-mindedness of a certain kind of man of religion. The scene in which he mistakes the De'il for God and promises to shake P-P's spiritual pride represents a successful matching of legend, fantasy, and social satire. Dr. Pothecary moves appropriately from her rôle as witch-doctor in the coven scene to that of psychiatrist and apologist for science and scientific method. Ketch succeeds more as a figure on the naturalistic plane than as a stock character: he is a proletarian with a grouse, a political extremist, not without a touch of humanity in his protective attitude towards Baby. He is most vividly portrayed as a type, as a false prophet, when he expresses his credo in the argument with Beadle in Act II.

Joe Mascara, "Joey", is the most colourful and complex

of the seven prophets. As Ursula Gerber points out, he has something in common with Shakespeare's clowns in the way he makes his ironical and cynical comments. He plays a dynamic part in exposing and denouncing the wickedness and stupidity of the two arch false prophets Ketch the Communist and Beadle the Churchman; and his function as Shakespearean clown-chorus figure is underlined by his 'arias' or 'songs'—dramatic monologues flavoured with Scots that combine a rhetorical quality with low comic touches. In one of these, his serenade to the lamp-post in Act II, he comments ironically on the dilemma of Pounce-Pellott or the archetypal figure he represents:

> Pilate, wi' hinging lip and sweet urbanity,
> Has come a second time to judge humanity.
>
> Dod, and he'll mak a bonny moagger o't, as he
> Done afore . . . But whit was he to dae?

On the naturalistic level he is a character in his own right. He is the artistic sensualist scornful of the Minister's pomposity; he is the opportunist ready to teach Baby the ways of sex; and he is the anarchist admitting no laws or rules except those that gratify self. The part he plays in the fantasy as Devil's stage-manager announcing the De'il and bringing in the Maiden for her initiation anticipates his attempted seduction of Baby in Act II. If anyone plays the Devil's Deputy throughout the play it is Joey—as character, mouthpiece of a hedonist philosophy, sardonic clown, false prophet. At the end Bridie makes P-P stress Joey's evil influence—the more evil for being negative, infertile, unorganised:

> Your harp has made the Halls of Tara

103

An intellectual Sahara.
I do not want you, Joe Mascara.

The remaining two of the seven prophets are more slightly drawn and only loosely fitted in to the naturalistic-legendary weave of the play. Robert Copper features briefly in the Prologue as Policeman but does not appear as a real character until the second act. Here he is the link between P-P's past life in India and his present life in Baikie. He is characterised as the Civil Service type and the representative of a blind belief in authority. In the debate he emerges as a hide-bound administrator with a vague belief in 'experts' and the working of democracy. Lady Maggie in her vagueness and inconsequential chatter is a comic figure on the periphery representing the past and the outmoded aristocracy. In her references to things past and people dead she links her naturalistic character with the figure of the Ghost in the legend. As a witch in the Devil's fantasy speaking Scots, she slips appropriately into a Scottish setting of folklore and the supernatural.

Because of the central importance of the figure of Pounce-Pellott-Everyman and Bridie's presentation of the seven prophets as contemporary deadly sins or evil influences, *The Baikie Charivari* may be regarded as an experiment in applying the Morality technique to a contemporary situation. It is possible to argue, however, that Bridie, in elaborating the parts the seven play and in developing their naturalistic characters, has blurred or even destroyed his Morality or Miracle pattern. This seems to be the view of T.C. Worsley in his review of the play in *The New Statesman and Nation* in October 1952. Worsley wrote of the "false starts and dropped herrings", "entertaining analogies", and interruptions that "smudge the lines"; but he added that Bridie had provided "a more enjoyable evening in the theatre than most playwrights give us". On the other hand, it is equally possible to argue that Bridie has enriched and developed the Morality element in *The Baikie Charivari* to give us a human rather than a strictly moral or divine interpretation of the problem of Everyman. A comparison with Marlowe's *Doctor Faustus* may be useful here. Faustus was tempted by his devils and gladly succumbed, glorying in his power and vanity one moment, terrified by the prospect of eternal damnation the next. Marlowe presents his intellectual Everyman in his moral predicament; and there are signs that he was trying to break out of a traditional mould that kept men's minds fixed in the narrow conventions of the mediaeval concept of man's relation with God. *Doctor Faustus* ends however with an unambiguous divine judgment: Faustus is punished by everlasting death and damnation. This makes good theatre but remains conventional Morality practice. On the other hand, the very fact that the seven false prophets in *The Baikie Charivari* represent contemporary evils and contemporary characters keeps Bridie's play on a human level: at least we can say that his Everyman is tempted in human terms. In this respect he is the hero, the single figure assailed by a group. Faustus and Pounce-Pellott as chief characters would appear at first to have one thing in common— *hubris*—the weakness of the tragic hero. Faustus's pride is illustrated throughout Marlowe's play; Pounce-Pellott's pride is merely referred to at times—by the Devil and Beadle in the opening fantasy, and by Lady Pounce-Pellott in Act I when she sketches for Beadle her impressions of her husband's character. The whole structure of *The Baikie Charivari* reveals how P-P deliberately and systematically sheds his *hubris*. Despite the ironical overtones, P-P genuinely wants to divest himself of his power, his prejudices, his tendency to lay down the law: he wants to learn the new ways. His route to wisdom is not Lear's—not the physical and mental purgatory of storm and turmoil. His is the intellectual method, the way of debate, of listening to and sifting the evidence presented to him. He remains the judge, but he judges in a spirit of grace. It is not as a divine figure that he judges: it is as a human being aware of his own weaknesses. He rejects both Ketch and Beadle because they believe and speak in lifeless formulas; he rejects 'Doctor Jean' because she oversimplifies human make-up in terms of theoretical psychology; and he rejects Joey for the aridity of his selfish nihilist philosophy. Instead of being judged as Marlowe's Faustus is, Pounce-Pellott judges—before he gives himself up; and instead of being taken by the Devil he is to be left alone for a time, perhaps for ever:

De'il. I'm thinking you've jouked me for the moment. It may be you've jinked me a'thegither. Time will tell us.

The dramatic scheme of the play is therefore both derivative and original. P-P is Everyman who is tested and tempted; he is Faustus seeking knowledge and understanding, and pursued by a devil trying to bring him down through his spiritual pride. But the temptation scenes and the symposium, although they demonstrate P-P's ironical detachment, bring him to a final state of grace, humility, and righteous anger, rather than to a state of overweening pride. He is not punished for *hubris* but released for having avoided it, for having seen through, rejected and destroyed the false prophets. Indeed, it may be that Pounce-Pellott has more in common with Goethe's Faust than with Marlowe's Faustus—in his search after perfection, his rejection of the unsatisfactory, his renunciation of self, and the shedding of his pride. In the end, like Goethe's Faust, Pounce-Pellott is saved not damned.

The question may well be asked: does *The Baikie Charivari* work as a unity within its different planes? To answer this conclusively would require a detailed examination of the method and flow of the whole play; but at least we can view its general method and shape for possible clues as to how it operates as a unified work for the stage. The first transitions from fantasy to naturalism and to theatrical formalism in the Prologue are smooth enough: in the theatre we can accept the movement from the De'il's invocation to the realist dialogue between Policeman and Beadle, back to the fantasy of the De'il's impersonation of God, and finally to the choric formalism of P-P's address of identification to the audience. Act I up to the Devil's Initiation Fantasy also operates smoothly enough: the parade of the characters—an artificial feature in itself—is managed with some skill; and on the three occasions when the act breaks into verse—the Joey-Beadle duet on a sense of humour, Joey's little song "Jump into the Wind", and Beadle's rigmarole on the commandments—the switch to verse to expose character and false credo seems justified as an extension of the pattern. Certainly the fantasy at the end of Act I is well prepared for: P-P falls asleep by the fire, dreams the witches' initiation ceremony, and wakens in time to save Baby from "going to the Devil". Act II is more difficult to assess. There are frequent modulations from naturalism to formal soliloquy and transitions to front-stage acts and fantasies. The symposium itself is formally opened by a monologue in verse by P-P; it proceeds in a fairly naturalistic manner; but it formalises into 'songs' and 'duets'—mostly to throw up the antagonism between Church and Communism, or to give the clown as chorus a chance to satirise and universalise the argument. The play certainly reaches its great climax and dénouement in those

107

coups de théâtre in which P-P first rejects and then destroys the prophets; but I feel that Act II generally is too episodic in its sudden transitions from naturalism to poetic formalism, too slack in its control of the symposium, to impress by its dramatic design, although what appears episodic or slack in reader's theatre may turn out to be stimulating contrasts or necessary relaxations of pace or even effective experiments in masque technique in practical production. What there is no doubt about in my mind is that Bridie succeeds in bringing about a satisfactory ending. It is satisfactory because it is logical in an unexpected way: Toby is given the custody of the daughter—youth has been called in to restore the balance; and P-P, having judged others, offers himself for judgment but is found at least not guilty. (This, it will be noted, is the verdict Pontius Pilate passed on Christ.)

Pounce-Pellott's method of trial has exposed the prophets even if it has not presented a possible alternative to their philosophies; but in that we leave him still awaiting a reply there seems a note of optimism rather than despair. Helen L. Luyben goes further: she believes that P-P " . . . affirms a faith in a final purpose", and that "His disordered and destructive action testifies to a transcendent order . . . " That possibility remains; but Bridie's ending does not make it explicit. Indeed it seems to me that the play ends on a deliberate note of doubt and vague expectancy. Punch has again become Pounce-Pellott who fuses into Pontius Pilate still seeking truth. P-P has found no solution to his question, only false teachers with false dogmas and dubious remedies. The structure of the play suggests that its main message is an indictment of all existing political, religious and aesthetic theories, an indictment gradually built up within the consciousness of P-P as Everyman. P-P's desire to start all over again and his eagerness to know, stressed at the beginning of the play, are still there at the end, despite his disillusioning experience with the prophets who "did not know . . ."—

> . . . and no more do I . . .
> I must jest again and await my reply.

Under the irony and the jesting there may lie in that awaiting a hope of something better.

Each of these plays has at its centre a leading figure isolated from the other characters, some of whom, as we have seen, form a "chorus". Both central characters— Lady Pitts and James Pounce-Pellott—are presented from a variety of angles; and here Bridie's "poetic" method is seen in practice. Lady Pitts is first presented as a sage or a Cassandra offering her words of wisdom in her inebriate state, then in the middle part as the domesticated wife, hospitable and loving. A third angle is presented when she comes in contact with the poet and becomes the romantic succumbing to his influence. By yet another modulation or change of angle she becomes, by the power of Ernest's poetic imagination, the goddess remote, unattainable. In the same way Pounce-Pellott is viewed from different angles. He appears to us at first formally as the ex-governor come home to learn afresh; later he is the husband annoying and placating his shrewish wife; in the 'songs' and monologues he is the archetype behind the contemporary figure—Pontius Pilate home from the East after washing his hands of Christ. By a more violent modulation he becomes the legendary Punch, killing his assailants and asserting himself; but his return to the Miracle or Morality plane as Pontius Pilate at the end restores the balance within Bridie's 'poetic' structure.

Bridie's non-naturalistic use of minor or choric characters is an interesting feature of these plays. In

Daphne Laureola they appear as purely peripheral characters—a quarrelling couple, spivs discussing the next moves in their confidence games, young couples with little to do but observe and chatter, "knowing" ones like Gooch and Watson. These characters are there to comment on the action and keep us in touch with the ordinariness of life: we need not expect from them any real character studies or development. They are neutral figures who throw into relief the remoteness, the isolation and the suffering of the central characters Lady Pitts and Ernest. In *The Baikie Charivari* the seven prophets play a much more active part: they try to influence and corrupt the central character. They constitute the device by which he is tested. In trying to affect P-P's actions and thoughts they display the limitations of their own thinking. In the end they are revealed as types or even vices rather than personalities. In other words Bridie is not thirled to naturalistic technique in presenting and exploiting minor characters: in these mature plays he boldly reduces characters to ciphers or qualities or evil forces to make his commentary on society and mankind.

Both *Daphne Laureola* and *The Baikie Charivari* are experiments in superimposing non-naturalistic elements on an essentially naturalistic story and setting. The method used in *Daphne Laureola* is perhaps more subtle: modulation to prophetic commentary and mythological plane is contrived through heightened mental state rather than by means of any specially staged fantasy or dream. It is when Ernest and Lady Pitts are brought together and isolated by the intensification of the dialogue or when either becomes spiritually isolated from the group that the transition from realism to allegory occurs. This is in contrast to the method used in *The Baikie Charivari* where the non-naturalistic plane is externalised in fantasy scenes featuring the De'il and characters from the legend or folklore, or where the naturalistic scene is suddenly suspended or frozen, in the style of the masque as in *The Tempest,* to allow a character—Joey and Beadle in Act I, P-P himself in Act II—to come forward to perform an aria or song or vaudeville act that ritualises and deepens the thematic scope of the play. Whereas in *Daphne Laureola* the allegory and myth are kept to the dark backward of the intellectual sub-conscious, in *The Baikie Charivari* legend, myth and Morality are right in the forefront and are alternated with the naturalistic story. *The Baikie Charivari* may be the more experimental of the two; but both are deepened by these modulations from realism to allegory. It is in this structural aspect that one discerns something of a poetic method in Bridie's technique.

The language of these plays has a greater intensity than that of Bridie's earlier plays. *Daphne Laureola* still shows the author delighting in thin realistic dialogue to establish the ordinariness of life or to satirise lack of sympathy or communication; but in his treatment of Lady Pitts in her high moments he captures the prophetic note in language that has a kind of measured dignity and simplicity. Ernest's idealised impressions of Lady Pitts herself are similarly caught in a heightened but controlled form of language. As a contrast to these, Sir Joseph's words are crisp, dry, laconic. One might say that the language of *Daphne Laureola* is in black, white and grey tones, whereas the language of *The Baikie Charivari* is more variegated, with a range from the conventional grey of the domestic scenes to the harsh red and yellow colours of Joey's attack on Beadle, and the bright blue and gold hues of some of P-P's speeches. Bridie shows himself something of a virtuoso in his handling of language in *The Baikie Charivari:* in the fantasies he is capable of a swaggering diabolical Scots; in the symposium scenes he uses wrangling rather than rhetorical rhythms; and in P-P's 'arias' he achieves at times a lyrical note tempered by irony.

In both these plays Bridie is experimenting with dramatic techniques and language in order to express more cogently his ideas about human problems that are contemporary and universal. In *Daphne Laureola,* through allegory and myth he contrasts the ethereal and the earthy; and by the insecurity of his central character Lady Pitts he symbolises the insecurity of the contemporary scene. In *The Baikie Charivari* he uses the devices of the classical, mediaeval and modern theatre and music hall to point the dilemma of modern man beset by evils, seeking a breakthrough to a better way of living glimpsed at in the Christian myth. These two late plays afford proof of the virtuosity and high seriousness of Bridie as playwright.

PART TWO

Technique, Qualities, Achievement
of the Major Plays

Bridie's Achievement as Dramatist

CHAPTER FIVE

BRIDIE'S DRAMATIC CRAFTSMANSHIP

THE IMPRESSION THAT emerges from early reviews and criticisms is of Bridie as an intelligent, entertaining and stimulating playwright not often successful with final acts and with serious flaws as a dramatic craftsman. Despite the efforts of later more discerning critics, this impression lingers on. In *New Trends in Twentieth Century Drama* (1967) Frederick Lumley ends a two-page study which attempts to place Bridie's work in the context of modern drama with a graceful tribute:

His imagination, the sharpness of his intellect and the flow of his language . . . have assured Bridie his own place of honour in the theatre since Shaw.

Yet he too subscribes to the view that Bridie was an indifferent craftsman: "As so many critics have complained", he writes earlier in the article, "a play by Bridie has the appearance of being unfinished"; and he adds: "It is more like a first draft, often in urgent need of revision and structural alteration".

The survey I have attempted of the technique, structure and finales of these nine major plays will I hope in some measure correct this persisting impression. As a craftsman

Bridie is seen to be in the direct line from Greek drama with its use of chorus to interpret themes and throw the protagonists' struggles into high relief, from mediaeval drama with its concern for dramatising concepts of good and evil, and from Shakespearean romantic or tragi-comic drama with its concern for bringing out both the *agon* and the agony—the *agon* between two forces or personalities, the agony of a central figure who is yet saved from becoming the tragic hero in the full sense. More obliquely he reflects the influence of the comedy of manners—in his satirical references to Scottish society in such plays as *The Anatomist, Mr Gillie, A Sleeping Clergyman, The Baikie Charivari.* At first sight, his work appears to be rooted in the technique of social realism as developed by Ibsen and Shaw; but he is not really so much concerned with purely social and economic problems, although he does show the influence of the naturalistic play in his attempts to catch the authentic dialogue of ordinary people—Lowland Scots, Cockneys, bourgeois housewives. He is influenced by the disquisitory style of Shaw, not only in the obvious example of the Brains Trust play *It Depends what you Mean,* but in other more important works like *The Baikie Charivari* and *Mr Bolfry* where the argument is part of the framework of the play and where fantasy is used to sharpen the intellectual focus and heighten the drama. In his last plays, particularly *Daphne Laureola* and *The Baikie Charivari,* he shows the influence of the "poetic" method of Shakespeare, T.S. Eliot, and Ibsen, in his exploitation of allegory and myth, in his use of symbolism, and in the self-questing moral intensity of his protagonists. In his dramatic technique Bridie, although he begins by being thirled to the naturalistic West End style, reveals the spirit of the experimental artist trying out classical, traditional, and contemporary methods in an attempt to find his own style and express more cogently the ideas thrown up by his plays.

He is keenly aware of the importance of form, not constricting form but form that fits the theatrical medium and enables him to develop and illuminate his dramatic power. His use of a three-movement form—*aba* or *abba*—as in *Tobias and the Angel, The Anatomist, Mr Bolfry, Susannah and the Elders, Daphne Laureola*, enables him first to trace the development of story and character, then to highlight character change and illumine theme by returning the play to its base transformed by the experience of the middle movement.

By means of this ternary form Bridie is first of all able to contrast one setting with the other, one tone with the other, the realist or naturalistic mode with the romantic or fantastical mode, not merely for theatrical embellishment but also as a necessary development and expansion of the scheme of the play. The analogy with music helps: the change to a new mood or setting corresponds to the change to second movement or subject with change of key and tempo. *Tobias and the Angel* moves from the sober settled mood of its Nineveh setting to the passionate swiftly changing mood of the Hamadan setting at the centre of the play. *The Anatomist* moves from its respectable "Quality Street" setting to the emotional melodramatic settings of its middle movement. The physical setting of *Mr Bolfry* does not change; but the switch in tone or plane from the naturalistic to the metaphysical when Bolfry appears amounts to a change in mental setting; and the debate, intellectual and relevant to the characters and situation though it is, is the more striking for having as one of its protagonists a non-realist character. The change from legal tone to the romantic and menacing atmosphere of the Hanging Garden in *Susannah and the Elders* is made gradually, by a kind of bridge-passage modulation rather than formal change of setting. The change back to the atmosphere of trial scene is more sudden; but both gradual modulation and sudden change are felt as part of the pattern of a play that is concerned with the contrast between the official public image and the secret hidden impulses of man. Bridie uses the contrast in the two settings in *Daphne Laureola* to throw up the two aspects of Lady Pitts's character: in the restaurant setting she is a disintegrating personality offering her wisdom in an insecure world; in the garden scene she is the integrated lady of the house dispensing hospitality.

Secondly, Bridie exploits this ternary form for its cyclic effect. In *Tobias and the Angel,* Act III, we go back to the home territory of Nineveh, a home territory familiar in its essentials—the figures of the patient Tobit and the shrewish Anna, but transformed by the return of Tobias married, more mature, able to perform miracles. Even more important, this 'ordinary' setting is recognised by the end of the third act as a place set aside from the ordinary, a place that has been "visited" by a supernatural figure. When we return to the home setting of *The Anatomist*— the Disharts' drawing-room, we find the bourgeois calm replaced by the excitement of Knox's defiance amid threatened violence. The two contrasted moods—the conventional and the questing—are synthesised, or at least juxtaposed, in this third part, within the original setting. *Mr Bolfry* is constructed according to a variation of ternary form—the second movement is in two sections; but again Bridie in returning to the naturalistic mode of the first part transforms it, both by demonstrating character transformation (in McCrimmon) and by staging a little fantasy within the naturalism to strengthen the resolution (the umbrella trick). In *Susannah and the Elders,* despite its apparently episodic nature, there is a shapely return to the atmosphere and setting of a trial, only this time the mood is heavy with the possibility of real tragedy. The resolution comes about through Daniel's penetration to the truth by means of his legal re-presentation of the action of the middle part of the play; but the evil spirit of the garden hangs heavily over this final scene and its outcome. *Daphne Laureola* is set in the same variation of ternary form as *Mr Bolfry*; but its return to the original setting is more strikingly deliberate than in the others plays. The symmetry is effective in demonstrating theme and character development: Lady Pitts drinking brandies in the first part is balanced against Ernest drinking brandies in the final part; but the tranformation in Lady Pitts's situation and attitude is made the more eloquent and dramatic for being presented within the exact pattern of the original setting.

In this tendency to use a ternary form Bridie seems to be following the tri-partite division of a play into *protasis, epitasis,* and *catastrophe*—the so-called neo-Terentian pattern believed to have been the basis of Terence's comedies and traceable in many of Shakespeare's plays. In the change to a different world in the middle part and the return to a home or "court" base in the third we can also see something of Shakespeare's method—in his "green-wood" plays *As You Like It, A Midsummer Night's Dream, The Two Gentlemen of Verona,* in the "dark" comedies *Measure for Measure* and *All's Well that Ends Well,* and in the tragi-comedy *The Winter's Tale.*

Dr. Angelus and *Mr Gillie* are constructed for the most part as naturalistic plays restricted to one setting: on the face of it two late-period plays set in the straightforward conventional pattern of the three- or two-act twentieth-century drawing-room play. Although Bridie appears to be using ternary form in *Dr. Angelus*, he has not the advantage of a change of setting in the middle part for contrast and development as he has in the five plays we

117

have just considered. *Dr. Angelus* is interesting for the way the material is shaped and developed within each act rather than for any dramatic change of atmosphere or mood between the acts. In the first act Bridie uses the long speech, the monologue, to vary the mood or tone: in Johnson's recital of the Hippocratic Oath he has moved out of the naturalistic plane for the moment to present an idealist or timeless view of the practice of medicine, against which Angelus' intrigue and sordid actions later in the act make their own ironical commentary. In the second act we have a clearer illustration of Bridie's method of bringing about variety and contrast in tone within the naturalistic mould of the play. The realism of Angelus' acts is set ironically against his theorising on Bacon's Idols; and Johnson's credulity in accepting Angelus' explanations in realist sequences is thrown against his realisation of the truth in the dream fantasy. In a sense the structure of *Dr. Angelus* is similar to that of *Mr Bolfry* in that there is a swift modulation into a dream fantasy that throws up hidden truths, and in that this leads to a self-recognition scene. Indeed Act III in *Dr. Angelus* shows how far Bridie can move from the naturalistic plane while still operating within the same naturalistic setting. The *anagnorisis*—Johnson's recognition of the facts about himself, Butt and Angelus—is followed by the monologue pronounced by Angelus over Johnson's unconscious figure, a monologue in which the theme and motives for the murders are distanced, moved to a non-realist psychological plane. Finally, although it looks as if we are returning to a purely naturalistic mood or tone with the appearance of MacIvor, the police inspector, this character does dramatically fulfil the function of a *deus ex machina* in appearing at the end to bring about resolution and point the moral.

Mr Gillie is structured in binary form like *A Sleeping*

Clergyman, in two distinct acts within the same naturalistic setting. Also like *A Sleeping Clergyman* it has a kind of chorus device that introduces and comments on the action. But the chorus device in *Mr Gillie* takes the form of a fantasy that features representatives of God watching the progress of Gillie's life. The fantasy in its three sections—Prologue, Interlogue, Epilogue—introduces, separates, and completes the two main naturalistic parts of the play: its function, as we have seen, is to distance and comment on Gillie and his life, and to give judgment. But within the two main parts there are structural features that enable the play to rise above its naturalistic setting. In each half there is a build-up to an inner crisis at which Gillie expresses his credo in a dialogue with Gibb; and at the end of each half we see him putting his credo into practice. Another similarity can be traced between *Mr Gillie* and *Dr. Angelus*: the second half of *Mr Gillie* and the third act of *Dr. Angelus* unfold an *anagnorisis* in which the central figure (Gillie, Johnson) comes to recognise himself or his failings or the true facts of the situation.

A Sleeping Clergyman and *The Baikie Charivari,* basically also structured in binary form, are built up in short scenes or episodes rather than long acts. *A Sleeping Clergyman* in its first part moves from a concentration on its medical theme to a series of sordid acts that culminate in high melodrama. The second part moves from the personal and the sordid out to a concentration on the medical theme which is resolved in high romantic manner. The chorus figures Coutts and Cooper link the episodes and distance the theme; the figure of the sleeping clergyman and the character of William Marshall between them unify the play and symbolise the abstract notion behind its theme—the nourishing of the creative gene. *The Baikie Charivari,* coming at the far end of Bridie's career, does not have the high romantic optimism of *A Sleeping Clergyman;* but it has similar structural features. It moves freely and quickly from fantasy to realist sequence, from naturalistic episode to legendary episode, and is held together by *its* unifying figures—Pounce-Pellott himself and the De'il. The movement of *A Sleeping Clergyman* is towards preservation and salvation; that of *The Baikie Charivari* is towards rejection and destruction, rejection of evil doctrines and destruction of symbolic characters. Within the apparent pessimism of the ending of *The Baikie Charivari*, however, is a gleam of hope; within the apparent optimism of *A Sleeping Clergyman* is a shadow of doubt.

Something of the influence of the Mystery and Morality plays may be traced in these "binary" dramas of Bridie. *The Baikie Charivari* has behind it the story of Pontius Pilate; and it has temptation scenes as well as a parade of characters representing abstract ideas. *A Sleeping Clergyman* exploits the figure of the clergyman wholly as an abstraction (God) and that of Marshall partly as an abstraction (God's deputy); and both plays by their melodramatic style throw up notions and figures of good and evil.

The ambivalence which we have noted in the endings of *A Sleeping Clergyman* and *The Baikie Charivari* is an important aspect of Bridie's dramatic craftsmanship. At the end of *The Anatomist,* amidst an atmosphere of menace and uncertainty, a detached confident note is struck in Knox's concluding lecture. *Susannah and the Elders* ends on Daniel's gloomy note of self-questioning: alongside his triumph is set his doubt about the rightness of the action and the outcome of the trial. *Mr Bolfry* ends with McCrimmon humbled and the company shaken, but with Mrs McCrimmon making light of it all. *Mr Gillie* ends with the schoolmaster optimistically starting all over again after the collapse of all his hopes. *Daphne Laureola* ends with the shattering of all Ernest's ideals, but his restatement of the myth brings back something of his original idealism. *Dr. Angelus* ends with just punishment for the criminal and a promise of leniency for the innocent young doctor. *Tobias and the Angel* has a completely optimistic ending without a shadow of evil; but in its sense of wonderment it leaves us with a feeling of something not quite understood. Bridie's endings then, although they are structurally sound in their resolutions, have nothing of finality about them, no sense of solution or complete triumph or tragedy. This is a mark of their strength, although it has been seen as a weakness by the critics who have complained of Bridie's final acts. These endings often make a thought-provoking concluding but inconclusive commentary on the theme. We are again reminded of the Shakespearean method. *Twelfth Night* and *As You Like It,* perhaps also *The Tempest, Measure for Measure* and *All's Well that Ends Well,* have within their structural completeness a feature or a feeling of incompleteness, a problem unresolved, a character who has not fitted in— Malvolio, Jaques, Sebastian and Antonio, Lucio, Parolles.

As a balance to this ambivalence in his conclusions Bridie often uses distancing devices that enable us to see the problem, view the theme, consider the *agon* or the agony, coolly, in detached manner. Of the nine plays we have examined, four have prologues or choric devices that show the influence of the classical or Elizabethan theatre. Perhaps the least detached is the prologue to *Susannah and the Elders,* the Argument presented by a Reader who introduces the story, and hints at its serious theme in his concluding caution. A few years earlier Bridie had opened *A Sleeping Clergyman* with a 'Chorus' consisting of the two doctors Coutts and Cooper who review the story of the Camerons with conversational informality, seeing it as a completed whole and introducing it in the flash-back manner. This chorus returns to introduce Act II, anticipating the climax of the Great Epidemic, and referring only briefly to the figure of the Clergyman as "he stirs in his sleep". This seems to me a very effective and sparing use of the chorus. There is no return to it at the end, for in Marshall we have a character who takes upon himself both the choric function of Coutts and Cooper and the symbolic force of the sleeping clergyman. The urbanity of the Judge in the Chorus to *Mr Gillie* sets the tone of detachment so necessary and appropriate for a judicial assessment from above of the actions and beliefs of Gillie, who himself keeps his distance from life through his ironical detachment. This Chorus, appearing at the beginning, middle and end of the play, is characteristic of Bridie the comic dramatist who sought to see things in perspective and judge men coolly and justly. The chief character in the Prologue to *The Baikie Charivari* is the De'il who opens the play with an apostrophe to Baikie. This prologue is comparatively long and varied: the De'il reappears as God inciting the minister Beadle to expose Pounce-Pellot and shake his spiritual pride; and later he returns as himself, narrowing the focus of his function to present what is to be the high theme of the play—the testing of P-P and the attempt to bring him at last to hell. The diabolic note is struck very strongly in this prologue; but the De'il's reappearance in the final scene of the play in which he refuses to take P-P to hell after all shows him as a choric figure capable of making his own judgment coolly like Bridie's other choric characters.

Bridie's use of the De'il at the end of *The Baikie Charivari* has something of a *deus ex machina* effect: the De'il here has become something of an artificial device produced to bring about a resolution and a commentary. Inspector MacIvor appearing near the end of *Dr.*

Angelus fulfils the same function, as we have seen. Bolfry himself, appearing in response to the incantation in the middle of the play, has also something of the quality of a *deus ex machina*: his commentary on the young people has a certain theatrical piquancy. But he is too closely connected with the chief protagonist McCrimmon, too obviously interwoven with the moral and religious motifs of the play, to be regarded as a purely detached choric figure.

Bolfry is in fact more representative of another dramatic device used by Bridie: his metaphysical nature is exploited to intensify the dramatic situation and theme. To see Bolfry and McCrimmon together, to hear them debate on heaven and hell and preach for the souls of the young people, is to become more intensely aware of the beliefs and predicaments of McCrimmon himself as minister and human being. This Bolfry scene is one of the best examples of Bridie's use of the fantasy for dramatic intensification of theme. Another occurs in *Dr. Angelus* when Johnson falls asleep and has a vision of a trial in which he is accused of complicity in Angelus' crime. This fantasy not only demonstrates Johnson's inner dilemma but paradoxically brings him to clearer sight than he enjoys in the naturalistic scenes. Another striking use of the fantasy device occurs at the end of Act I of *The Baikie Charivari:* the build-up to the initiation of Baby at the witches' coven is a heightened illustration of the dangers that beset Pounce-Pellott's daughter in the real contemporary world.

Johnson's fantasy in *Dr. Angelus* is induced by drink. Elsewhere in these nine plays there are examples of Bridie's exploitation of the drunken state to present the inner truths of themes or motifs—a device that brings out his Scottish quality and links him with the MacDiarmid of *A Drunk Man looks at the Thistle.* In *A Sleeping*

Clergyman Dr. Marshall in Act I Scene IV (the Hannah-Wilhelmina scene) in semi-inebriate state blurts out to Hannah his hopes and fears for Wilhelmina and the future of the Camerons. In *Daphne Laureola* we have perhaps the most spectacular examples. Lady Pitts speaking through her double brandies tells the truth about her aspirations as a young girl, her desire to know about good and evil; and in snatches of song and in dialogue with Ernest she reveals something of the truth about her own broken-down state in a disintegrating world. In *Mr Bolfry* too there is a strong suggestion that the fantasy may have derived some of its power from McCrimmon's reversion to the whisky drinking he had given up in his youth. In *Susannah and the Elders,* at the beginning of Act II, as the company are drinking after the feast at the Hanging Garden, Dionysos' description of the uninhibited love behaviour of Greeks after feasting is also spoken in drink; and its heightened language hints at the passion and suffering to come: "—heaping up a jargoning delirium—torturing the body—tormenting the soul".

These moments when the theme is laid bare or an aspect of character revealed or a penetrating commentary made on the high theme occur elsewhere in Bridie's plays without the influence of drink, when the protagonist is carried away by the flow of the dialogue or debate to express his own enthusiasms or beliefs. A moving example occurs in *The Anatomist* near the end of Act III: Knox's love for Amelia and Amelia's sympathy have prepared the way for a moment of frankness when Knox admits his responsibility for the murders—his soul is "sick . . . at the horror" he has done. Similarly, McCrimmon in the humility of his self-recognition near the end of *Mr Bolfry* admits he was too proud of his intellect. Gillie in a more challenging mood expresses his credo, as we have noted, at two moments of inner crisis in a debate with the minister

Gibb. Susannah's short prayer just after sentence has been passed on her is perhaps a more muted example of how a moment of inner crisis brings out the protagonist's credo. In *A Sleeping Clergyman* the central theme of the play is beautifully summed up in Marshall's *nunc dimittis* lines expressing the old man's vision that concludes the play. In *The Baikie Charivari,* in Pounce-Pellott's soliloquy after he has been tempted by Jemima Lee Crowe, Bridie uses the resources of irony and lyricism to point the thematic relevance of the temptation and its rejection.

It could be said that these nine plays provide us with a portrait gallery of interesting, sometimes fascinating Bridie characters; but we would be left with a very narrow view of the scope of his plays if we limited ourselves to a study of his charcter drawing as such. Despite the fact that he wrote some parts with certain actors or actresses in mind, his characters have generally a significance beyond any idiosyncrasy exploited or personal part played. (This is not to deny the power of the character drawing in such parts as Harry Magog in *Gog and Magog* and Donald MacAlpin in *The Forrigan Reel.)* That is why it is pointless to look for rounded characters all the time. True we have some first-rate satirical portraits. Davie Paterson, the janitor in *The Anatomist*, is a truly comic portrayal of the Scottish hypocrite, a study to be placed alongside Burns's Holy Willie; but the portrait is firmly integrated into the scheme of the play—by the confrontation with Knox and by the part Paterson plays in the melodrama of the mortuary. Bridie's satirical power is also at its sharpest in his picture of the Walkers and their snobbery in *A Sleeping Clergyman,* and in his exposure of the treachery, sentimentalism and hypocrisy of Dr. Watson in *Mr Gillie.* But again these are carefully set in the context of the plays: the Walkers' snobbery is thrown against Cameron's dynamic forthrightness; Watson's treachery is thrown against Gillie's objective belief in mankind. Bridie's housewives are not always "the key to the whole business", as Mrs McCrimmon seems to be in *Mr Bolfry:* Anna in *Tobias and the Angel,* Mrs Gillie, Judy in *The Baikie Charivari,* are all variants of the shrew type tailored to enable them to fit into the individual pattern of the play.

It is when we move to the central figures that we see something of Bridie's own method, his originality in the creation, development and manipulation of his characters. There is an intellectual restlessness, a high seriousness, a concern with values professional or moral, that give the portraits a Scottish intensity. The most arresting examples are McCrimmon and Gillie who are absorbed in the intellectual aspects of their professions. McCrimmon combines a delight in the dialectics of divinity with a strict authoritarian attitude towards its morality. Gillie has the greatest contempt for conventional ideas on education and for the day-to-day drudgery of school teaching: what excite him intellectually are the creative aspect of education and the creative urge in art. Johnson in *Dr. Angelus* is a less impressive disciple of high seriousness: for one thing he is too inexperienced; for another he is up against a dynamic apostle of evil who can act the angel plausibly. All the same, Dr. Johnson's own brand of high seriousness is vividly illustrated in his attitude to the Hyppocratic Oath and in his self-recognition and courage in facing the consequences of his unwitting support of Angelus' crimes. The best examples from these plays of medical men as central figures of moral intensity are Knox in *The Anatomist* and the Camerons in *A Sleeping Clergyman.* Knox is driven on by his passion, an almost religious passion for anatomy. The Camerons are driven on by their absorption in the work of isolating bacilli and devising serums to destroy these. These characters are tempted by evil or tainted with evil; but equally they reveal an awareness of the evil within their own natures and a kind of missionary zeal to benefit mankind. On the one hand they are open to the forces of good and evil; on the other they are seekers after the medical Holy Grail.

This moral preoccupation in Bridie's characters may well be attributed to his Scottish background and culture— particularly the influence of Presbyterian principles; and it explains why we have to think of some Bridie plays as Moralities. Perhaps his medical and professional characters best illustrate this passion; but there are others who are driven by a similar moral urge. Susannah for all her friendliness and playfulness emerges as the Puritan and the highly religious Jewess, firm in her belief in the ultimate justice of God. Her broader humanity contrasts with Daniel's fanatical belief in the chosen people. Daniel is driven on by his narrower nationalist-religious passion. As a Scot, Bridie can understand the concentrated passion of a patriot whose way of life has been threatened, just as he has sympathy for Susannah as the patriot trying to understand her enemies. The tragedy of Lady Pitts is that she has lost her moral drive: we have only illustrations of it from her past life in the first restaurant scene, and an impression of it when she plays the faithful wife in the garden scenes. Ernest Piaste is more of the seeker after the Grail—in his belief in education, in his search for the ideal. This Polish displaced person, uncertain of himself and yet intensely caught up with his Presbyterian form of religion and his pursuit of knowledge, reflects something of the Scottish psyche. In Pounce-Pellott we have the archetypal seeker after wisdom. In the seriousness that underlines his detached irony, in his tussles with the De'il, in his awareness of the seven deadly sins personified by the Seven Modern Prophets, he is a variant of Everyman placed in a Scottish setting and surrounded by the rhythms of the Scots tongue.

Frequently Bridie uses his subsidiary characters as choric figures. Characters like Mary Belle, Amelia, Walter, and Raby in *The Anatomist,* the Walkers in *A Sleeping Clergyman*, the young people in *Mr Bolfry,* Mrs Gillie, Tom, Nelly, Watson and Gibb in *Mr Gillie,* step down from a partially realised individuality to become part of the crowd, the chorus who comment, criticise, and throw into high relief the dynamicism of the chief character. By the end of *The Anatomist* Mary, Raby, Walter and Amelia have become part of the admiring crowd of Knox; by the end of the third scene of *Mr Bolfry* the young people have become a very subdued chorus; and the Walkers after their commentary in Act II of *A Sleeping Clergyman* are dismissed to the background of the play. Bridie thus shows a tendency at various points in his career to exploit minor characters as choric figures; but it is only in his last plays, particularly *Daphne Laureola* and *The Baikie Charivari,* that he fully develops and utilises this theatrical device. The subsidiary characters appearing in the first, second and fourth acts of *Daphne Laureola* are for the most part chorus figures, recapitulating the situation, commenting on and giving information about the main characters. Their chorus function is emphasised deliberately by stylised repetition of pattern in dialogue and setting—particularly in the first and last acts. The seven subsidiary characters in *The Baikie Charivari* are individualised more sharply and have more to do in the action and development; but they too are chorus figures in that their function is to throw the emphasis on the character and moral progress of the protagonist himself. Some of the prophets come to life as individuals or types— Ketch as contemporary politician, Beadle as pompous clergyman, Pothecary as lady doctor or psychologist. Others play their parts more as stock figures like Joey the

Clown, Maggie the Ghost, and Jemima Lee Crowe the Temptress with the American gold. These figures are 'paraded', presented at times more like abstractions in a Morality play; and at the end they are forced formally to take their place in the chorus, a legendary chorus that is violently dismissed by Pounce-Pellott himself.

The Scottish tendency to develop the *alter ego* or *doppelgänger* feature in literature has already been commented on. I conclude this commentary on Bridie's dramatic craftsmanship by indicating how this feature may be traced in his method of characterisation. Dr. Robert Knox is both angel and devil—the angel seeking to serve humanity and the devil conniving at murder to maintain the supply of "subjects". Raphael plays the lowly porter to Tobias, but we are often made aware, sometimes comically, of his higher *alter ego,* the proud angel behind the pose. Both Charles Camerons lead double lives—as dissolute young men and as doctors of genius. The Elders pose as respectable Assyrian judges but reveal themselves as lascivious goats, just as Angelus poses as a medical angel and reveals the calculating (and lascivious) devil underneath. Lady Pitts is the gracious lady and the loving wife; to Ernest she is the goddess; but deep down she is an ordinary earthy creature who needs a keeper. The best example of this *alter ego* feature in Bridie is however the one in *Mr Bolfry.* That portrait of McCrimmon-Bolfry is an achievement to be placed alongside Hogg's Wringhim and Burns's Holy Willie.

CHAPTER SIX

BRIDIE'S LANGUAGE

AN EXAMINATION OF these nine plays gives us an opportunity to observe Bridie's handling of language at close range. At a first hearing we might be inclined to criticise his dialogue for a stilted quality perceptible in *The Anatomist.* In the theatre I have sometimes been made aware of the artificial ring about parts of the opening dialogue:

> *Amelia.* I have heard you sing better, Mary Belle.
> *Mary.* I know. I am in poor voice tonight. I don't know why.
> *Walter.* I thought you sang it with great feeling and expression.

* * * * *

> *Walter.* Don't go abroad, Miss Amelia . . . I think the evenings are more beautiful in Scotland than anywhere else in the whole world.
> *Amelia.* In the whole world, Walter? You must be the great traveller to pass your judgments on so wide an area.
> *Walter.* Well, I have been to Calais and to Madeira.
> *Mary.* You are quite the Christopher Columbus.
> *Walter.* And you are suddenly very waggish. I rejoice to see you have become sprightly again.
> *Mary.* I rejoice, sir, in your rejoicings.

It may be that Bridie is here deliberately attempting to catch something of the tone of Edinburgh polite society of the earlier nineteenth century, not merely as an ironical

Barrie pastiche, but also for a serious dramatic purpose. The cosy "Quality Street" atmosphere and the douce Dishart sisters are to be violently contrasted with the harsh events and characters in the middle section of the play; the reference to travel will turn out to be significant; and Walter's cliché "I think the evenings are more beautiful in Scotland" is to be echoed drunkenly in the sordid setting of The Three Tuns scene. But Bridie, successful in catching the genteel style, also developed an ear for loose colloquial dialogue and the inanities of conversation—near the opening of *Mr Bolfry,* as we have seen, and also in *Mr Gillie.*

In *Mr Gillie* some of the inanities of the dialogue between husband and wife, on the subject of the wireless licence for example, seem irrelevant as well. On the other hand, this kind of opening bout between Gillie and Watson does illustrate how Bridie can use snatches of conversation to suggest character and humorously lead up to a confrontation:

> *Mr Gillie.* . . . Besides, I want a crack with you.
> *Doctor.* I wanted to talk to you too.
> *Mr Gillie.* Good. What about?
> *Doctor.* Two or three things. Give me a moment to arrange my thoughts.
> *Mr Gillie.* Your thoughts are in some disorder?
> *Doctor.* They're aye that way. But thank the Lord I ken what to do for it. (*He helps himself to a stiff peg.*) What about you?
> *Mr Gillie.* Not yet, thanks. But help yourself.
> *Doctor.* I've already done so. But your permission will do for the next one.

This lightly comic passage is in striking contrast to the dialogue Bridie uses for more serious dramatic effects. In

Susannah and the Elders, following the scene of Susannah's agony—the attempted seduction and Kashdak's proclaiming her an adultress, there occurs in the trial scene a passage that illustrates a deeper quality and a skill in producing a powerful *coup de théâtre:*

> *Susannah.* ... O Everlasting Lord, receive my spirit!
> *(She sinks to the ground, supported by women and Joachim.)*
> *(The Judges are standing on either side of the inner gates. The tipstaves approach Susannah.)*
> *Daniel. (who has remained seated, now springs up and shouts in a loud voice)* I am clear of the blood of this woman!
> *Latazakar.* What's that? Who said that? Who are you, sir? What do you mean?
> *Daniel.* I am Belteshazzar, a Novice of the College of Justice.
> *Latazakar.* Be silent, sir.
> *Daniel.* In the name of the king! I've a right to be heard.
> *Latazakar.* This is very extraordinary. What have you got to say?
> *Daniel.* Latazakar, take your state and re-open the Court. If you will not listen to me, you will make yourself a derision and a hissing to the King and his people and to the multitude of their children for ever and ever.

In the later play *Daphne Laureola* Bridie seems able to combine this deeper quality with the trivia of conversation to give his colloquial dialogue power and relevance. Here is an extract from the first passage between Ernest and Lady Pitts:

> *Lady.* I lurk in the alleys. I am the prima ballerina of

the crumbling chimney stacks and the wet slippery slates. Did you drink my brandy?

Ernest. No, Madame.

Lady. I must have drunk it myself. You look honest enough.

Ernest. It is very kind of you to say so.

Lady. Are you a foreigner?

Ernest. Yes, Madame. At home I am not a foreigner; but now I have no home.

It will be realised too that the language here is strengthened by the metaphorical quality in the opening speech, a quality characteristic of the whole play.

From these examples it will be appreciated that Bridie is capable of a fairly wide range of dialogue styles. Even when he seems to be introducing unnecessarily the trivialities of conversation, we should suspend judgment for a little: he has generally a reason for these inanities; and frequently he shows a skill in using easy conversation to sketch character, build up atmosphere, and anticipate drama. He can also give us passages of dialogue that contrast one character with another to great dramatic, humorous and satirical effect. In this passage from *The Anatomist* he counterpoints Paterson's guttural dogged Scots with Knox's sharp impatient English:

Paterson. ... *(reading the Bible)* ... and ye shall sow your seed in vain, for your enemies shall eat it. And I will set my face against you ...

(A key turns in the lock.)

What's that?

(Knox comes in.)

(Rising) Ye frichtit me, Dr. Knox. You're early aboot the day.

Knox. Yes. *(He hangs his hat and cloak on a peg and*

133

takes off his gloves)

Paterson. I was expecting twa callants wi' a corpse.

Knox. Good.

Paterson. They was wantin' twelve pound for it, Doctor.

Knox. They were, were they?

Paterson. I'm feart we'll hae to pay.

Knox. Well, pay them, damn it.

Paterson. I havenae the siller by me.

* * * * *

Knox. . . . What's that you're reading? *(Picking up the Bible.)*

Paterson. It's lonely for me here. I was reading the Book. It's bread and meat to me is the Book.

Knox. You're a canting humbug, Paterson. There is poetry and philosophy here, but what do you know of poetry and philosophy?

Paterson. There's God's Word in it, Doctor. There's religion.

Knox. If they could cut out the religion it would be a more useful book.

(Knox goes out R, slamming the door behind him.)

Paterson. Aye. Bang the door. Ye blasphemious bitch!

This is the kind of passage that works effectively on the stage. Here we have tension, relaxation, deliberate structuring of the dialogue to display character in action, *and* a humorous conclusion that is the more effective for being in two overlapping parts.

Bridie shows similar power and versatility in his writing of long speeches. These can range from the flamboyantly rhetorical in *The Anatomist* and *Mr Bolfry* to the conversationally lyrical in *Tobias and the Angel,* from the conventionally legal and intensely religious outbursts in *Susannah and the Elders* to the pompously rhetorical style of *Dr. Angelus*. In *Daphne Laureola* the long speeches have at times a kind of apocalyptic power; in *The Baikie Charivari* they are heightened by being set in an impersonal lyrical mould. The rhetoric in *Mr Bolfry* is more ostentatiously intellectual than in *Mr Gillie* where the long speech has the quieter ring of the personal credo. First take this rhetorical outburst from McCrimmon in Scene I of *Mr Bolfry:*

You do not believe in Predestination? That is because you do not like it. If you only believe what is nice and comfortable, our doctrine is of no service to you. If I give you a crack on the head with a stick, you need not believe it; you need not believe in your dentist's drill or in the tax-gatherer's demand. Go on. Believe what is agreeable to you. I do assure you that you will be in such a continuous state of surprise that your eyebrows will jump off the top of your head. Even your heathen philosophers *knew* that Predestination was a fact, like Ben Nevis. You can go round it. You can go over it. But you are foolish to ignore it.

There is a great confidence about the rhythms here that brings out McCrimmon's delight in intellectual play on words and ideas. It is so carefully patterned that we are inclined to be suspicious: it seems to bring out a ministerial glibness in McCrimmon's character. Compare it with this passage from *Mr Gillie:*

Mr Gillie. ... I know the Community. The Community nowadays means Parliament and the Civil Service. We pay them to look after us, and so they do. In return we have to do what we are told, like the wretched brats in my school ... There's only one kind of man who isn't ordered about from the cradle to the grave, and that's the artist. He's bullied like the rest; but he's under nobody's orders. He's responsible to God and, perhaps to his neighbours. But not to what you call the Community. I'd be an artist myself if I could. If I can't, I'll help others to be that. And you and the rest of you can do what you like about it.

This is a more conversational kind of rhetoric, with less obvious pattern about it. It is more down to earth—the kind of style that enables the note of personal sincerity to emerge clearly and sharply.

Finally, let us take three examples of long speeches in Bridie that have an intense imaginative quality that extends the range of the thought, speeches that illustrate his ability to move to a non-naturalistic plane—psychological or allegorical or archetypal. First here is an example from Angelus' monologue over the recumbent body of Johnson, the monologue that under the guise of a hypothesis gives the psychological explanation for all Angelus' criminal acts:

Let us take a fantastic and laughable instance. Let us suppose that he is a doctor devoted to the study of his art and determined to take his rightful position as a benefactor to all mankind. He must have free play to the wings of his imagination. He cannot be cramped by the petty embargoes of a general practitioner's environment. Even the sanctions of his own earthly, animal nature tend to hold him fast to the ground and they cannot be allowed to do so. Suppose this man to have made an unfortunate marriage. Suppose him to be subjected to the incessant attempts of two ignorant and narrow-minded women to mould him to their miserable conception of what a right-thinking domestic animal ought to be. At every turn they trip him with their beastly apron strings. They are forever trying to lower him into that barber's chair where Samson, Judge of Israel, was shorn of his strength. Suppose this man to have passionate physical longings. Unless they are satisfied, he cannot plan, he cannot think, he cannot invite his soul, he cannot rise above the earth. Above all he cannot make his wretched female gaolers understand his necessities. What is he to do?

Compare this with a speech by Lady Pitts in *Daphne Laureola,* Act I, where in pessimistic mood she presents in turn a child's apocalyptic view of *The Tempest* and her adult apocalyptic view of the decline and underlying corruption of civilisation:

My father took me to *The Tempest* as a great treat when I was nine years old. It wasn't a great treat: it was a terrible nightmare. It was about an old scientist on an island. He had a daughter who was almost an imbecile. He had a slave called Caliban. He tortured poor Caliban with rheumatism and frightened him with spangled spooks. After twenty years on the island he sailed away and left it worse than it was before. No books, no spooks, nothing but rheumatism and Caliban in a bad temper. Caliban got two masters. One was drunk and the other was silly. I don't know what he did with them after the liquor went dry. He probably ate them. Thank God the play stopped before that. It always happens. It always happens. "An hundred generations, the leaves of autumn, have dropped into the grave". And again we shiver miserably in the confines of a long winter, as Christendom and the Roman Empire did hundreds of years ago. Again and again and again and again we have covered the face of the earth with order and loveliness and a little justice.

137

But only the face of it. Deep down below the sub-terranean brutes have bided their time to shake down our churches and palaces and let loose the little rats to sport among the ruins.

Now consider this extract from Pounce-Pellott's introductory ode to the symposium in Act II of *The Baikie Charivari*. Here P-P, by fusing his own past life as governor with that of the archetype Pontius Pilate, makes his own dilemma the more vivid, dramatic and universal:

To a vast, ancient land,
Made ours by cunning and courage and force of arms,
They sent me, Pontius Pilate, to teach and to rule.
They chose me from many.
I was packed full of meaning.
I knew self-denial.
They sent me to teach and to rule.
To school the men of the East to seek and to find,
To invent and manipulate,
And to rule themselves, when the Great Day came,
The Day when the passion of the West found its
    apotheosis,
When the dragon was cast down and death and Hell
Cast into the lake of fire.
"Now", said we, "by precept and example
"We have shown you how men rule themselves.
"Take back your land and our God be with you.
"As ever He is with us".

So Pilate is home again, his occupation gone.
Bewildered by change and frightened by the lingering
    sharp smell of ashes.

Be kind to him and take him by the hand.

Guide him through the Millennium.

Within the patterned rhetoric of the Angelus passage one is aware of a rising rhythm excited and personal despite the impersonal guise. In the use of emotive words like "ignorant and narrow-minded women" on the one hand, and "benefactor", "free play", "wings of imagination" on the other, there is discernible the egotistical note that comes to its high point when the *persona* behind the psychological struggle is equated with Samson. Thereafter the pace quickens with the series of short sentences until the personal dilemma is reached and summarised. The *Daphne* passage seems at first simpler and more straightforward, more staccato, appropriate to the exploration of the child mind. But as the message broadens, the language expands, the sentences become longer and more rhythmic, forming a suitable verbal vehicle for a vision, Lady Pitts's apocalyptic vision of a disintegrating civilisation that she herself represents in her own situation and state. The *Charivari* passage has a direct but impersonal quality that suggests the legendary. Behind the measured simplicity of the words describing P-P's rule over an alien people, its rhythms recalling those of the prose psalms, lie commentary and dry satire; and in the imagery of the dragon and hell there is a kind of prophetic power. The change to quoted speech enables the playwright to present the official expression of the political act with formal, religious gestures; and from here we return in the last few lines to the high themes of the play—P-P's personal dilemma and the dilemma of Everyman who needs guidance in a bewildering new world.

An examination of these three extracts reveals not only the versatility of Bridie in handling language, not only his virtuoso performances in handling different kinds of verbal rhythms, but also an awareness of the power of some of the devices of poetry—metaphor, allegory, vision, and consciously patterned language.

Although Pounce-Pellott is made to speak in English throughout *The Baikie Charivari*, in this play Bridie uses Scots more frequently than in any of the other plays we have examined. In the Prologue the quality and intensity of the Scots used by the De'il vary. His first soliloquy has an echo of the T.S. Eliot style (in "The Fire Sermon" from *The Waste Land,* for example) that seems to prevent it from going more fully Scottish:

> A slate-grey township . . .
> And Scots baronial mansions
> Handy by train for the City,
> For shipbuilders, stockbrokers, wholesale grocers to
>   die in,
> Lulled by the wash of the waves of the Clyde
> And soothed by the sicht of white sails and the cries of
>   the seabirds—
> Baikie, my own, my Beloved,
> No sae genteel, these days, no sae genteel.

His second soliloquy (near the end of the Prologue) is more strongly Scots and has an echo from the ballads:

> I maun get me a hantle mair hellhounds to fill up my
>   pack,
> And he'll gie us a run for our money. He'll gie us a run;
> But we'll chase him and catch him and pu' him doon, ere
>   the long day is done,
> Hoho, hoho. The cock doth crow.
> Fiat, fiat. I go. I go.

Beadle in the Prologue speaks a Scots that occasionally recalls Burns; but basically this seems to be a couthie sentimental variant specially tailored to reflect the character:

Aye, he's honest eneugh and what for no?
Cantie and douce in cosy bit hoose
Wi' a decent like spouse and a bairn to cheer him
And naething ava in the warld to steer him.

In the fantasy at the end of Act I Bridie reverts more to the Scots of the ballads. The language here has the earthy vigour and strongly marked rhythms of folklore: its incantatory style and its special lexis— "cummer", "widdershins", "carline"—make it an appropriate vehicle for diabolical intrigues:

Cummer, go ye afore. Cummer, gae ye.
Gin ye winna gang afore, Cummer, let me.
Linkin, linkin widdershins,
Ring-a-ring a-widdershins,
Cummers, carline, crone and queyn,
Round gae we.

To mark the change from fantasy to realism and from naturalism back to fantasy, Bridie makes some of his characters switch from Scots into English and from English back to Scots. Pothecary and Lady Maggie both revert to Scots in the fantasy, and this reversion seems natural enough for these characters. In making Baby revert to Scots, however, Bridie may be commenting satirically on language usage in Scotland: the clipped Anglo-Scottish tones she would use in the naturalistic scenes may be intended as a humorous contrast to the broad Scots she uses in the fantasy. Underlying the oscillation from a standard or imposed linguistic form to a more basic and natural one, however, may be a more

141

serious purpose. Bridie may be using Scots in *The Baikie Charivari* to reveal the sources of our impulses and the reservoirs of our personality, and to uncover some of the secrets of the psyche hidden by the veneer of civilisation.

Linguistically *The Anatomist, A Sleeping Clergyman,* and *Dr. Angelus* are what might be called middle-class Scottish plays: the speeches and dialogue of the main characters may occasionally reveal a Scottish quality, but more strongly marked Scottish linguistic features are to be found in the speech of the servant or "lower" classes. In *The Anatomist* Bridie uses a fairly powerful Scots to convey the character and personality of lesser mortals like Davie Paterson and Mary Paterson who feature in the melodrama of the middle movement. Earlier in this chapter we noticed how he throws the Scots of Paterson against the English of Knox to great comic effect; and we may note how in the same play Mary Paterson is made to switch suddenly from an angry kind of urban Scots directed at the Landlord and Paterson to a more sympathetic kind of proverbial Scots in her scene with Walter. Mary's Scots is worth examining for its pace and colloquial flow which is sometimes held up by a touch of the genteel as in the use of "mooshwar" in this passage:

> Puir wee thing wi' your mouth a' treacle and your tail a' parritch and your heid a' wumps! What are ye greetin' for? . . . That's not genteel. Dry your eyes on your mooshwar and sit up like a wee gentleman.

Mary Paterson's language may be set alongside the kind of language the Disharts' maid Mary Ann uses:

> Michty, this is a bonny like home-coming frae foreign parts. But it's a God's mercy you're safe. I'll hae a tassie o' tae ready for ye in a jiffy. It's on in the

142

kitchen, and I brocht some griddle scones for ye, Miss Amy.

This is vigorous but plain colloquial Scots: there is no touch of the genteel here. The word "tassie", despite its French origin, is thoroughly at home in its context; and the placing of expressions like "michty", "bonny like", "God's mercy" within the rhythmic flow ensures a characteristic Scottish panache.

In *Mr Bolfry* the linguistic situation is reversed. Here it is the main characters—the McCrimmons—who show the influence of Scots, and the subsidiary characters—the young people (apart from Morag the Highland maid and Cohen the Cockney)—who speak standard English. The Minister and his wife are given well-patterned language that owes its quality and attraction not only to a combination of Lowland and Highland rhythms but also to a strongly marked Scottish idiom. Here is McCrimmon holding forth on the uneducated English:

They are so ignorant that their own Episcopalian meenisters, poor bodies, in ministering to them have wellnigh lost the power of human speech. I have to wait till I see Father Mackintosh, the priest from Strathdearg, before I can converse in a civilised language forbye the Gaelic.

We have here examples of Scots usage—"poor bodies", Scots pronunciation—"meenisters", and Scots idiom—"forbye the Gaelic"; and the flow of the second sentence, structured by its special syntax—"wait till . . . before"—is unmistakably Scottish. Mrs McCrimmon's language is, if anything, even more colourfully Scots, especially when she is emotionally stirred. Here she is holding forth on her reactions to being bombed:

... There's whiles I can frighten myself more than Hitler or Goering and that lad Rommel could do if they were all in this room waving their pistols and making faces at me. I'll be lying awake at night with my head under the blankets thinking there's devils and bogles and kelpies coming down the chimney, though fine I know there's no such thing. But when they dropped a big bomb in Aberdeen and me at a shop door and knocked over with the blast with all my messages flung mixty maxty, I wasn't afraid at all, at all. I was just angered.

From the opening to the ending the Scots idiom is there: "There's whiles ... I was just angered". The use of the future continuous tense is characteristic; and there is a Scots proverbial quality about the breathless syntax of "there's devils and bogles and kelpies ... ", and an illustration of the colloquial force of the absolute construction—"and me at the shop door ... " The whole passage has a rhythmic continuity that is typically Scots.

Bridie does tend in some of his plays to use Scots conventionally—for comic purposes and restricting it to the lower classes; but even where he does this, it is obvious he has a keen ear for Scottish idiom and sentence pattern. In a play like *Mr Bolfry* he can demonstrate the full power of Scots by putting it into the mouths of his main characters. Here he is beginning to experiment with its special qualities in an attempt to portray Scottish character and insight. It may be significant that he uses Scots more consistently in his last play *The Baikie Charivari* than in any of the others. He had used Scots and Scots verse in his first play *The Sunlight Sonata* (1928) which he called a "Farce-Morality" and which has obvious parallels with *The Baikie Charivari*—a devil figure and a parade of abstract characters. His return to the old language at the end of his career with greater confidence and zest would seem to indicate a renewed faith in it as a linguistic and literary force of great dramatic potential.

CHAPTER SEVEN

BRIDIE'S ACHIEVEMENT AS DRAMATIST

I BEGAN THIS study by grouping the three plays in my first chapter under the title "Three Doctor Morality Plays"; and subsequently I found myself facing a Morality pattern in the other plays under examination. This points to Bridie's preoccupation with moral values and his tendency to reproduce some of the features of the mediaeval moral play. The Doctor Plays present notions of good and evil: they are concerned with the struggle of a Dr. Everyman against evil within or outside himself, and his struggle to pursue his medical work for the good of mankind.

It is however not only in the "Doctor Moralities" that Bridie shows the influence of the mediaeval play. In *Susannah and the Elders* his method may be different: he does not present his good and bad angels so obviously; but the moral power is felt throughout the action. As the Elders are revealed in all their wickedness, Susannah rises to the heights of her moral integrity; and if we wanted to point to the presence or activity of a Good Angel, we have the intervention of Daniel in the final scene to save Mrs Everywoman and to bring retribution to the forces of evil. In *Tobias and the Angel* the conflict between good and evil is formalised in the pantomime that illustrates Raphael's superiority over Asmoday. In this play the Good Angel has all the advantages, including intelligence and good looks. Here, too, we are concerned with a kind of moral pilgrimage: we watch Tobias's gradual transformation from raw youth to mature man under the guidance of Raphael as Knowledge. Even if the Morality method is not so evident in *Mr Gillie,* Gillie himself can be regarded as an intellectual Everyman resisting the influence and

146

efforts of those who would corrupt him into accepting conventional notions of morality. *Mr Bolfry* becomes almost pure Morality in its middle movement: Minister and Devil are theatrically juxtaposed and their credos contrasted; but this part of the play eventually becomes more of a psychological Morality as the argument reveals the close identity of Minister and Devil. If anyone plays the Good Angel in *Mr Bolfry,* it is Mrs McCrimmon dispensing tea and drawing the domestic moral at the end. By the end of *Daphne Laureola* Ernest may be said to have escaped the possible corrupting influence of Lady Pitts as Lady Sensualitie but he goes on worshipping her from afar. He is more the idealist Everyman cutting himself off from common humanity. In *The Baikie Charivari* we have the clearest example of Bridie's Morality pattern: the ironic Sir James Pounce-Pellott-Everyman is tempted by the Seven, exposes the falsities of their remedies and 'beliefs', and in the end faces the possibility of spiritual death in his confrontation with the De'il but is saved by the moral power of his own beliefs and actions.

A strong moral compulsion then runs through the works of Bridie; and it seems to me that one of his achievements in drama is to fashion his own particular type of Morality to make his comment on the medical world, on professional life, and on contemporary society.

Although there is an intensity in this preoccupation with moral values, we have noted that there is never a clear-cut solution, an unambiguous ending, the black-and-white triumph of good over evil. In *Mr Bolfry* we have the clearest example of his interest in the idea of the universe as a pattern of reciprocating opposites of good and evil. One of the main purposes of the debate between Devil and Minister is to demonstrate precisely that thesis. But elsewhere Bridie reveals how fascinated he is with the idea. The three doctor plays present the evil alongside the good, or the good emerging from the evil, or the good almost submerged by the evil. In *Susannah and the Elders* the evil is seen simply as the other side or the lower half of human nature: the respectable judges can change to lascivious goats. By studying *Daphne Laureola* we realise how closely this pattern of reciprocity is allied to the characteristic Scottish delight in contrasting the base with the beautiful: the beautiful and remote goddess Lady Pitts can be transformed to Mrs Vincent feeling safe and protected in becoming part of ordinary humanity. In *The Baikie Charivari* the contrast of the base and beautiful is at its sharpest in Pounce-Pellott's ironical commentary after his temptation by Jemima Lee Crowe in which the beauty of the East is set in a context of vulgar commercialism.

Two other contrasts in Bridie's work are to be noted. On the one hand he deals with the dark forces of life and nature, on the other with the higher powers of the mind—dialectic, argument, vision—using the resources of poetry to illuminate his ideas—symbolism, metaphor, myth. We have seen how he weaves the ingredients of real-life Victorian melodrama into his Doctor Plays: here he is interested in exploring the dark recesses of the criminal mind and sexual aberration. Some of these problems are explored also in *Susannah and the Elders*. More important, he reveals the traditional taste of the Scot for the supernatural and devil lore, and an interest in those aspects of our nature that these things lay bare. His handling of the divine supernatural in *Tobias and the Angel* is graced with wit and urbanity; his intellectual impression of the devil in *Mr Bolfry* emerges theatrically out of the mediaeval apparatus of witchcraft and spells; and his treatment of the De'il in *The Baikie Charivari* owes something to Scottish folklore and ballads. Even in a naturalistic play like *Mr Gillie* Bridie shows his delight in the supernatural as a theatrical device which can extend and enrich the scope of the play.

As a contrast or sometimes as a complement to these illustrations of the deeper or darker forces of life and nature, Bridie presents his illustrations of the intellectual forces within us. At the heart of some of his plays he sets a debate or symposium: those in *Mr Bolfry* and *The Baikie Charivari* are the outstanding examples; but there are arguments and discussions in the other major plays such as *A Sleeping Clergyman, Susannah and the Elders* and *Mr Gillie.* This represents another Scottish characteristic— a great love of argument, although as a playwright Bridie may have been influenced also by the example of Bernard Shaw. Bridie's arguments sometimes dissolve into flyting— that peculiarly Scottish form of verbal brawling that goes back to the Scottish mediaeval poets—the Makars; but there is no doubt that he himself took his debates seriously. Indeed, his interest in ideas and the need to debate them is a hallmark of his work; and he himself seems to have believed that this was related to his Scottish make-up. At the end of his Preface to *Susannah and the Elders and other plays* he referred to "the little theological discussion" he wrote for the opening of the new Broadcasting House in Glasgow (his play *The Kitchen Comedy* 1938) and said he had heard of one group of English listeners "whom it reduced to tears and boredom". On the other hand, he added, this kind of debate "is the kind of thing that Scotsmen of the proper sort can hear enraptured all night". He might well have added something about the moral intensity with which ideas are expressed and debated by Scotsmen, the kind of moral intensity that gives his own plays their special quality. The Camerons in *A Sleeping Clergyman* are obsessed with a belief in the supreme importance of their medical work; Johnson in *Dr. Angelus* is fanatical about the need to accept responsibility for what he thinks is his own moral lapse in supporting Angelus; Susannah never wavers in her belief in the goodness of God. In *Daphne Laureola* we have the reverse side of the coin: it is the lack of moral purpose in Lady Pitts that brings about her tragedy; it is the lack of moral purpose in civilisation that is causing it to crumble into ruin like the restaurant. *The Baikie Charivari* reveals this moral drive more subtly and more strikingly than does any other Bridie play. Under his urbanity and irony, his good manners and child-like desire to learn afresh, Pounce-Pellott builds up an impression of a man driven on by tremendous moral passion, capable at the end of destroying the forces of evil that would corrupt him, capable of acknowledging his own moral lapses, and capable of going on waiting and hoping.

One would not normally associate strictly poetic qualities with Bridie's plays; and certainly in the absolute sense, in the sense that T.S. Eliot and Christopher Fry are poets as well as dramatists, one could hardly claim that Bridie was a poet. Yet, as we have seen, there is a sense in which he seemed to be moving towards a poetic method in his later works. Even in early plays like *A Sleeping Clergyman* and *Tobias and the Angel* he was aware of the power of music or song in building up atmosphere; and in *Susannah and the Elders,* as we saw, he was beginning to experiment with the poetic device of symbolism—the symbolism of nature in particular. In later plays like *Daphne Laureola* and *The Baikie Charivari* he builds his symbolism—the symbolism of myth and legend—more closely into the fabric of his work. In this respect he may well have been influenced by the example of Ibsen and Shaw—the Ibsen of *The Wild Duck, A Doll's House, The Master Builder,* the Shaw of *Heartbreak House.* In the final play *The Baikie Charivari* he is experimenting with verse itself—rhymed and unrhymed, and with the rhythms of folklore and ballad, in an attempt to extend the dramatic range.

If not in the absolute sense, certainly in the subtleties of his method, attitude, and experimentation, Bridie then can be regarded as poet and artist. Our study of *Mr Gillie* proves how close he comes to understanding the artistic viewpoint and credo. From Shakespeare, as we have suggested, he appears to have learned something of dramatic method; and in his later works he becomes more and more interested in trying out different kinds of writing, different styles in English and in Scots, from the mundane to the visionary, from the argumentative to the "poetic" and the revelatory.

Time has gone on and ideas have changed since Bridie wrote his last play. We have had new schools of dramatists, new fashions in drama. We have had the Drama of Disillusionment, the Theatre of the Absurd, Anti-theatre, the Drama of the Little Man crushed by the forces of society and the state, the Theatre of Menace and Despair, Kitchen Sink Drama. The difference between Bridie's plays and plays of the fifties and sixties may be accounted for by the changing *zeitgeist*. By the time Beckett wrote *Waiting for Godot,* Wesker *Chips with Everything,* Pinter *The Caretaker* and *The Birthday Party,* man had shrunk still further within his world of bombs, bureaucracy and boredom. His frustrations eventually robbed him of his power to communicate, but not at first. There is nothing inarticulate about Osborne in *Look Back in Anger:* very eloquently he represents Jimmy Porter's frustrations, frustrations that resulted from an unnatural uprooting of working-class people through an arid educational process. Although there are similarities, the difference between this outlook and Bridie's may be accounted for in terms of different

151

national cultures. The essentially working-class viewpoint taken by Osborne, and later—in their more menacing studies of inarticulate people—by Pinter, Wesker and Beckett, tends to be bitter and sectarian. Something of the disillusionment that comes with loss of national greatness as well as a sense of the littleness and helplessness of contemporary man may also be in it. The Scot on the other hand has never been as fully committed to the idea of Empire although he helped the English to build up theirs. He has never fully accepted ideas of class distinction; and, because of his moral intensity, he is perhaps slower to accept the notion of the helplessness of man. He therefore only partly reflects the disillusionment and the narrow working-class viewpoint. Bridie, although he presents his ideas from a middle-class angle, frequently satirises the pretensions, humbug, and hypocrisy of that class. He never in himself reflects its prejudices or superiority or arrogance. On the contrary, in *The Baikie Charivari,* we have the supreme example of Bridie's declassed Everyman testing every pretension from whatever stratum of society and finding it wanting. In his continuing belief in mankind— in salvation through medical research and education, in his rejection of dogma in politics and in the Church, above all in the moral and intellectual drive that he demonstrates throughout his plays, Bridie is essentially the Scot at his best, independent in his thinking, concerned with moral values rather than class prejudices, resilient rather than pessimistic. He is typically Scottish too in his humorous treatment of religious problems—personifying and intellectualising the De'il, humanising an Archangel.

It has been said that Scotland owed its cultural greatness before the Union to its ties with European art and thought. Perhaps, then, it is significant that Bridie derives his strength as a dramatist from his links with Greek and mediaeval drama and with English drama of the

Renaissance which owed so much to Italian and classical sources. It is clear too that he owes something to the influence of an Irish dramatist and a Norwegian dramatist who broke away from contemporary moral conventions and fashions. Within the form that he carves for himself out of an experimentation that takes him back to the wellsprings of drama and forward to new techniques, and deriving his dynamic and inspiration from his Scottish background and traditions, Bridie has contrived to express some of the great problems and dilemmas of humanity from a characteristically Scottish viewpoint. When his work has been fully re-assessed it is possible he may be placed alongside Shaw, Brecht, Anouilh, Giraudoux, Fry, O'Casey, O'Neill, Williams, Miller, Wilder, Eliot, Osborne, Beckett, Wesker, Pinter, Dürrenmat, Ionesco, Bolt, Whiting, Arden, Albee, as one of the significant dramatists of the twentieth century.

Baldwin, T.W.: *William Shakspere's Five-Act Structure.* University of Illinois Press, 1947.

Bannister, Winifred: *James Bridie and his Theatre.* London 1955.

Barrie, J.M.: *Dear Brutus.* London 1939.

Barrie, J.M.: *Quality Street.* London 1918.

Brown, George Douglas: *The House with the Green Shutters* (first published 1901), edited with an introduction and notes by J.T. Low 1974.

Bridie, James: *Babes in the Wood.* London 1938.

Bridie, James: *The Baikie Charivari* with preface by Walter Elliot. London 1953.

Bridie, James: *Colonel Wotherspoon and other plays (Colonel Wotherspoon, What it is to be Young, The Dancing Bear, The Girl who did not want to go to Kuala Lumpur)* with a preface. London 1934.

Bridie, James: *Daphne Laureola.* London 1949.

Bridie, James: *Dr. Angelus.* London 1950, reprint 1955.

Bridie, James: *The King of Nowhere.* London 1938.

Bridie, James: *Mr Gillie.* London 1950.

Bridie, James: *Moral Plays (Marriage is no Joke, Mary Read, The Black Eye)* with preface "The Anatomy of Failure". London reprint 1949.

Bridie, James: *One Way of Living.* London 1939.

Bridie, James: *Plays for Plain People (Lancelot, Holy Isle, Mr Bolfry, Jonah 3, The Sign of the Prophet Jonah, The Dragon and the Dove).* London 1944.

Bridie, James: *The Queen's Comedy.* London 1950.

Bridie, James: *A Sleeping Clergyman and other plays (A Sleeping Clergyman, Tobias and the Angel, Jonah and the Whale, The Anatomist, The Amazed*

Evangelist). London 1934.

Bridie, James: *Susannah and the Elders and other plays (Susannah and the Elders, What Say They?, The Golden Legend of Shults, The Kitchen Comedy)* with a preface. London 1940, reprint 1943.

Bridie, James: *Tobias and the Angel* with introduction and notes by A.C. Ward. London 1931, reprint 1968.

Bridie, James: *Mr Bolfry* with introduction and notes by J.T. Low. London 1978.

Butler, Geoffrey L.: *Madeleine Smith.* London 1935.

Diack, Hunter: "The Theatre" (article on *Dr Angelus*) *The Spectator* Vol. 179, p. 173, Aug. 8, 1947.

Duke, Winifred: *Madeleine Smith* a tragi-comedy in two acts. Edinburgh and London 1928.

Fleming, Peter: "The Theatre" (article referring to *The Anatomist*) *The Spectator* Vol. 101, p. 589, Nov. 5, 1948.

Gerber, Ursula: *James Bridies Dramen* Schweizer Anglistische Arbeiten Bern 1961.

Goethe, Johann Wolfgang von: *Goethe's Faust: the original German and a new translation and introduction by Walter Kaufmann.* Doubleday & Co., New York 1961.

Heiberg, Hans: *Ibsen: A Portrait of the Artist* translated by Joan Tate. London 1967.

Hogg, James: *The Private Memoirs and Confessions of a Justified Sinner* edited by John Carey. London 1969, paperback 1970.

Ibsen, Henrik: *Peer Gynt* translated by William and Charles Archer Vol. IV: *The Collected Works of Henrik Ibsen* with introduction by William Archer. London 1907.

Ibsen, Henrik: *Hedda Gabler, The Master Builder* translated by Edmund Gosse and William Archer Vol. X: *The Collected Works of Henrik Ibsen* with introduction by William Archer. London 1907.

Jesse, F. Tennyson: (ed.) *Trial of Madeleine Smith*. London, Edinburgh, Glasgow new edition 1927, reprint 1949.

Kerr, Walter: "The Stage" (article on *Daphne Laureola) The Commonweal* Vol. 52, p. 630, October 6, 1950.

Lyndsay, Sir David: *Ane Satyre of the Thrie Estaits* edited by James Kinsley. London 1954.

Lumley, Frederick: *New Trends in Twentieth Century Drama.* London 1967, reprint 1969.

Luyben, Helen L.: *James Bridie: Clown and Philosopher* University of Pennsylvania Press, Philadelphia 1965.

MacDiarmid, Hugh: Essay on The Caledonian Antisyzygy. *The Scottish Chapbook.* February 1922.

Marcel, Gabriel "Le Théâtre de James Bridie" (essay referring to *Mr Gillie) Etudes anglaises* TX No. 4, Paris 1957.

Marlowe, Christopher: *Doctor Faustus* edited by John D. Jump. London 1962, reprint 1973.

Michie, James: "A Question of Success" (article on *Mr Gillie) English* Vol. XVII, No. 98. London 1968.

Mill, Anna J.: *Mediaeval Plays in Scotland*. Edinburgh 1927.

Pritchard, Dr. E.W.: *A Complete Report of the Trial of.* Edinburgh 1865.

Stokes, Sewell: "The English Spotlight" (article on *Dr. Angelus) Theatre Arts,* Vol. XXXI, No. 11, p. 47, Nov. 1947.

Weales, Gerald: *Religion in Modern English Drama.* Philadelphia 1961.

Wittig, Kurt: *The Scottish Tradition in Literature.* Edinburgh 1958.

Worsley, T.C.: "The Last Bridie" (article on *The Baikie Charivari) The New Statesman and Nation,* Vol. 44 (new series), page 448, October 18, 1952.